ROSES TO RAINBOW

ROSES TO RAINBOW

My Dog Gus in the Afterlife

REBECCA SCHAPER

GREYHAWK

Copyright © 2025 by Rebecca Schaper

All rights reserved. No part of this book may be reproduced in any form or by any electronic or mechanical means, including information storage and retrieval systems, without written permission from the author, except for the use of brief quotations in a book review. For permission requests, contact the publisher:

GreyHawk Media
635 Brisbane Manor
Alpharetta, GA 30022
books@rebeccaschaper.com
www.rebeccaschaper.com

Print ISBN: 978-0-9992771-6-4

Library of Congress Control Number: 2024927372

Kindle ASIN: B0DT7J9RSP

EPUB ISBN: 978-0-9992771-7-1

Book design: La Puerta Productions

Editor: Gerald Everett Jones

Copyeditor: Jason Letts

Proofreader: Adero Joan Cate

Author photo: Marion Yarger-Ricketts

All photographs are by the author except as noted in captions.

In Memory of Call and Gus

Beyond all I see through the eyes of my brother and the soul of my beloved dog, they have inspired this book and my healing mission.

1
GRIEF AND ANTICIPATION

This book is a memoir of profound loss, animal communication, and spiritual growth. You may be holding it because you are somewhere in that first phase. A beloved companion has passed out of your life. You're heartbroken, confused, and perhaps even angry. I don't expect your journey to be the same as mine, and I'm not sharing what follows as a model or as advice. I don't even expect you to buy into everything that I experienced.

I will simply tell it as honestly and as sincerely as I can.

My beloved Gus poses proudly with me at our beach house in South Carolina.

The passing of my sweet dog Gus was not the first sudden and shocking death I've experienced. Both of my parents died by suicide — at different times. My mother's tragedy became an unbearable trauma in my brother Call's life. Not long after discovering her sprawled out in the kitchen, he left the family home and was out of touch with us for nearly twenty years. This isn't my first book. I told the story of how Call came back into my life — and how he became something of a guru to me before he left it — in *The Light in His Soul: Lessons From My Brother's Schizophrenia* (also a documentary titled *A Sister's Call*).

I don't fear death. And I don't fear attending someone — human or animal — as their soul leaves their body. It's such a sacred time. What I feel in those moments is not grief but intense compassion as I focus on their distress and try to comfort them.

No, my heartbreak comes later, when I sense the gaping void they've left.

Then, there's what comes next!

May you find in these pages peace — and hope.

HIS EARTHLY LIFE WITH ME

In his earthly body, Gus was a wirehaired Vizsla, a centuries-old breed of hunting dog, a kind of pointer. Traditionally, these dogs are native to Hungary. The older of our daughter Kim's two dogs is a Vizsla by the name of Tucker, and she came to know the foremost breeder of these exceptional dogs, Zsófi Miczek, who has a farm and kennel outside Budapest.

Years back, my husband Jim and I had two dogs, who have since passed from our lives. We're well aware that being the guardian of an animal requires not only love and care but also commitment and diligence. When you take on that responsibility, you must be aware that your dedication to its caregiving must last for the duration of their life — or yours. And now that my husband and I are older, we understand the seriousness of adopting a being whose potentially twenty-year lifespan will outlast ours — or who deserves our full attention when we might not be physically able to give it. We were also aware that we could adopt an older dog as a rescue. But if there were complications and we couldn't cope, we would never return a dog to a shelter. Simply stated, even though we yearned for the companionship and love of another dog, we didn't want a new responsibility.

Nevertheless, Kim sensed something. She is an incredibly disciplined person herself, having overcome a series of dire challenges, and today she is a stellar holistic wellness coach. So, when Kim tells you to do something, you do it!

One bright morning seven years ago, she called me to insist: "Mom, y'all need this dog!" By "y'all," I knew she meant both me and Jim, and by "need," she was saying it wasn't an option.

In following Zsófi on Facebook, Kim had seen a photo of a young rust-colored Vizsla — no longer a puppy, but weaned and trained. He wasn't from a new litter. He was already eight months old. And the reason he was not yet adopted? A future as a hunting dog was not for him. In her words, "He's not a workaholic!"

Previously, Gus (which was not yet his name) had been sent to a buyer in England, who decided not to keep him. Zsófi's professional ethics prevented her from disclosing the reason to us, but we had to assume that this dog simply refused to hunt.

So, Gus wasn't a rescue, but as a stalker, a pointer, and a retriever, he was unwanted. Now, this isn't to say no one was interested in adopting him. The other common trait of Vizslas is their gentle behavior when they are not out in the field, making them ideal family members.

I looked at the photos Zsófi had posted to Facebook, then I showed Jim. We could see something in the face of this dog, and without putting it into words, we could understand at a deep level why Kim had urged we take him. Well, other people must have been attracted as well. As a favor to Kim, Zsófi had said she'd give us first refusal, but since others were interested, she wasn't willing to wait forever for our decision.

By the time Jim and I agreed we were willing to take this step, we had just ten minutes to make the decision. We were in a bidding war for a dog!

We went for it. For him.

Zsófi ships dogs all over the world, on direct flights whenever possible. Gus had to travel from Budapest Ferenc Liszt International Airport to Hartsfield-Jackson Atlanta International Airport. Even when the prevailing headwinds aren't strong, the flight time is over twelve hours. And even for a young dog who has been appropriately sedated, that must be a stressful journey. Gus had already undergone more than the usual transfers from one home to another, and we were worried how well he'd endure the trip.

But as it happened, Jim and I couldn't go to pick him up. On the day of Gus's arrival, we had to be at our beach house. So Kim's friend Ryan, who had experience being a caregiver for her Vizsla, went to the airport to meet the dog. Ryan kept Gus at his place overnight, and we worried again how confused this young dog might be when he finally met us.

We were worried there would be some separation anxiety, and he did seem disoriented at first. Getting here was a trial, for sure.

But one look at Gus dissolved all my fears. Zsófi had given him a Hungarian name, but that old-soul face told me he'd be mine by any name. I figured he'd had other names in other lives, and to me might as well be Gus. Some mothers of precocious children remark they were born forty. Gus was such a wise one. To me and to everyone who met him afterward, the name fit.

Zsófi's cryptic remark — "He's not a workaholic!" — was another indication of his mellow character. We thought she was implying he wouldn't hunt, but as he settled in with us, we realized his calm demeanor conveyed self-confidence and peace. Again, he was so young, yet so old.

Early on, we took him to our beach house. It was another plane ride — but this time, it was brief, and he spent most of the trip on my lap.

No sooner did we get to the house than he darted to the beach and jumped into the water. He swam like he'd done it before. (Indeed, we learned there was a pond at Zsófi's farm, and part of their training was to go into the water.)

He owned that beach. It was his place, and he couldn't wait to walk or to run. If I'd stop to talk with a neighbor or greet their dog, Gus would start spinning in circles. In his excitement, he wanted to keep moving.

His sense of ownership extended to dogs we'd meet. He was always the unquestioned alpha. He was never mean to them, but some he didn't approve of. Although Gus was usually curious, he remained aloof whenever we encountered a certain Golden Retriever, even though he was submissive to Gus. Like I said, he was never mean, only indifferent.

Some other dogs would bark at him, as if challenging him to a tussle. He'd just look up at me. Sometimes he'd sit down on the spot, as if to say: *Are we going to put up with this?*

But then toward other dogs — and other beings — Gus acted like a caregiver. One Doberman Pinscher, named Gracie, became a playmate of his. She was partially crippled from a back injury, and her movements were awkward. She could walk, but she couldn't run and jump. Gus was always careful around her. After conversations with Gracie's owners, I learned they wouldn't allow other dogs near her, fearing she could be injured if their play got too rough, but they made an exception for Gus when they saw how gentle he acted around her. The dogs' companionship led to something remarkable. Even though Gracie got walked frequently at the beach, her family was sure she hated the water, but Gus must've known otherwise. Haltingly at first, he led her into the surf, just enough to get her paws wet. Then, cautiously but insistently, he waded into the water, and eventually she followed. They ended up swimming together. Somehow, he knew the water would be soothing for her. Back on the sand, he'd sit down alongside her as she rested from the exertion.

Gus demonstrated reverence for the corpse of this dolphin.

On another walk, we encountered the beached corpse of a dolphin. Gus circled the animal's body, then he stood still. While I was gazing at the deceased dolphin, deciding what to do, I looked down and saw Gus lying right beside it. It was as if he was grieving along with me. I took out my phone and called the authorities. They said they'd come to take the body to the lab, try to find out the cause. I could tell Gus was glad I did something about it.

Sometimes on our walks, I'd stop to marvel at something. (I'll tell you about some of those times.) If I lingered and Gus sensed I didn't want to walk just then, he'd lie down and wait. He sometimes even took a little nap.

I felt he was teaching me patience. He was ever in the moment. He was energetic when it was time to play, but when playtime was over, he was never in a hurry. He insisted I slow down.

We have a pool at the house in Atlanta. There was no keeping Gus out of it. In the mornings, he'd jump in, then I'd towel him off. Jim and I called it his morning dip. Especially during the hot summer days, he'd swim in a circle to cool off, much as he'd spin around to show his excitement when we were walking on the beach. He had the run of the yard, yet he couldn't stay out of that pool. I indulged him, faithfully rubbing him down after each dip — sometimes four or five times a day! At first, I was worried this would be a chore. Then I realized he was giving me the gift of his joy. I never tired of doing things for him.

As many dogs no doubt do, Gus would be the first to sense that a package had been delivered at our door. When we were in the yard, I'd tell him to go get it. He'd run up the steps and put it in his mouth. I'd tell him to go put it on his bed, and he'd take it right there. So, when he looked at me with his ears cocked as though listening carefully, I never doubted he understood every word I said.

Gus was also sensitive to the rhythms of Jim's day. My husband has a habit of taking a brief "man nap" at one o'clock. And when the time came, whatever we were doing, Gus would run up to join Jim and settle down alongside him.

When we were in the yard or at the beach, I'd ask him, "Do you want to dance?" And like a dashing leading man in some old movie, he'd first take a bow! Then he would sit up and offer me his paw, as if graciously taking my hand. We'd then prance around joyfully. What a gentleman!

Gus's devotion to me was deep, heartfelt, and unwavering — his sincere gaze at me said it all — but the behavior of his that made him seem almost human was his love of Stella, Kim's older dog, a Labradoodle.

This dog often stayed over with us, and from the first moment Gus caught a whiff of her, they were inseparable until their next reluctant parting.

This dog often stayed over with us, and from the first moment Gus caught a whiff of her, they were inseparable until their next reluctant parting. Not similar breeds at all, they were both compatible and complementary. They were so comfortable with each other, you'd think they'd been lovers in past lifetimes. It wasn't torrid physically, more like an old married couple or a devoted brother and sister.

Gus, the old soul, was mellow in his demeanor most of the time. Oh, he was joyful and enthusiastic when he was playing, but he was never irritable. Stella, on the other hand, was something of a drama queen. She liked being served. At our house, we had a box full of toys for Gus. Of these, his favorite was a little lamb we called Yam. He'd bring Yam to bed with him, and it was touching to see how he used his precious toy to bond with Stella. As soon as she would show up, I'd call out, "Gus, find Yam!" He'd dig deep in the box and bring it out, then was quickly at her side with Yam in his mouth. The lamb became her favorite, as well, but she would enthusiastically tear it up, so we had to buy several incarnations of Yam for him to give her. His favorite toy at the beach house was Kitty Kat, which he also shared on Stella's visits, but he'd greet everyone with this toy, and he'd curl up with it at night.

Stella also gets hyper-excited when she sees or even catches a whiff of a squirrel, a chipmunk, or a mole — of which there are many in our yard. In a word, she's *gamey*, as they say of dogs trained to hunt. As I've said, Gus was never a hunter. If he had been, he'd never have come to us. That fellow in England would be tramping around some forest with him. But two dogs who are close tend to train each other. Gus was so attentive to Stella, he'd do whatever she liked, always seeming to guard her as well in the activity. So he joined in when she chased those little creatures. They never killed anything. Indeed, I don't think either of them would have known what to do if they caught one.

I love to dance and Stella loves to hunt. Gus took his greatest joy in pleasing us both. Seeing them together made me think of my caregiving for my disturbed brother Call, who passed from this life years ago. But, as I have written about him, during the ten years after he came back into my life from a long absence, his fraught mental state also gave him uncanny spiritual insight. I came to regard him — and I still do — among my spiritual mentors and guardians. When I see a hummingbird, he's paying me a visit, watching and listening as he hovers nearby. And as Gus does, and you shall see in the episodes that follow, Call sometimes sends me hawks with messages.

Gus's passing was sudden and unexpected. I first sensed something was wrong one morning after he and Stella had been playing hard in the back at our house in Atlanta. I took them for a ride in my car during my errands. Both were in the back seat, where of course they preferred to be, paying more attention to each other than to me. Returning home, when I stopped in the driveway and opened the car door, Gus didn't wait for Stella but jumped out right away, then he just sat down. He was very still.

Stella looked bewildered. She didn't know what to make of it. He should have been chasing her into the yard.

He was so still, not acknowledging either of us, staring into space.

I thought right away, *Something's wrong.*

I walked slowly over and opened the front door. Stella immediately bounded out of the car and raced in. Gus continued to sit there for a moment, then he got up slowly and followed me in. Stella was already in the kitchen. She probably thought it was time to eat. Still ignoring her, Gus walked up the stairs to where Jim was sitting in his study and rested his chin on Jim's lap.

I said to Jim, "Something's not right."

Jim nodded in agreement as he stroked Gus's head, saying, "Let's just wait until tonight and see. Maybe there's no need to be worried."

But I said, "No. I'm sure something is not right!"

I insisted on taking Gus to the emergency vet right away. Jim said he had a task to finish, then would bring Stella and follow in his car.

In the short time it took to drive to the vet, Gus was noticeably weaker, sprawled in the back seat by himself and not looking out. I called to alert the vet we were coming, and when we arrived, an attendant came right out to carry Gus in.

I stayed by his side as he lay on the exam table, where they did an ultrasound, which showed blood had pooled in his abdomen. They started an IV and gave him a transfusion.

All through this, I was touching and stroking him, talking to him to soothe him. There was some anxiety in his breathing, but he didn't budge as they probed him and stuck him. He lay there patiently, as if to say, *Do whatever you need to do.*

About an hour after the transfusion, they did another ultrasound, more thorough this time.

They found a tumor on his spleen. The doctor said they needed to operate.

Meanwhile, Jim had arrived in his car. We wouldn't be able to stay with Gus during the surgery, so he suggested we go back home. I'd been with Gus for hours, and Jim could see I was stressed. He thought taking a shower might help me calm down, and neither of us wanted to leave Stella in the car for very long.

So we went home.

I had stepped into the shower. Hot water was pouring over me as the steam rose. The sensation might have calmed my body, but my mind was racing. I kept telling myself, *He's in good hands! The best care! He will wake up and it will all be well. I'll care for him and he will heal quickly. He's a young dog. It's going to be all right!*

Jim ran into the bathroom to tell me Gus had died

on the operating table. Cardiac arrest during the procedure. Nothing they could do.

Gus had been eight months old when he came to us, and he was with us for six and a half years. Like I said, a young dog.

His time has come too early, I thought. I couldn't understand why.

We left Stella in the house, and Jim drove me back there. Neither of us said a word.

They had him wrapped in a blanket on that same exam table. They let me stay with him a long time.

As I've said, death doesn't bother me. I love being with a person or an animal during death because it's such a sacred moment, even after their soul has left their body. I still felt Gus's presence around me.

I just regret I hadn't been able to stay at his side. I felt it wasn't his time, but eventually he'd help me understand.

Even though I bravely say I don't fear death, my mind's understanding can't soothe the feelings of loss.

I was inconsolable after Gus's passing. It was about eight months before I could talk about him without getting so emotional. Jim let me have my space. I knew it had hit him hard as well, but he doesn't wear his emotions as close to the surface as I do. My memories of Gus are so vivid, and tears still come when I think of times we spent together at the beach.

We'd lost animals before, but this time the cut went deeper. I felt a part of myself had broken off. I suppose it was because Gus's sensibility seemed so human. An old soul. A teacher.

I admit that, after a time, I was looking for signs. And I won't disagree with you if you think I manifested them. The first seemed like a mere coincidence. One morning as I was checking my laptop, the word *bobblehead* appeared on the screen. I hadn't searched for anything like that, and it seemed to come out of nowhere. Bobblehead was my favorite nickname for Gus. His head was so big that it bobbed up and down as he walked, like a plow horse pulling a load, urging himself forward.

I thought it might be a sign from Gus, but as I said, I was looking for signs.

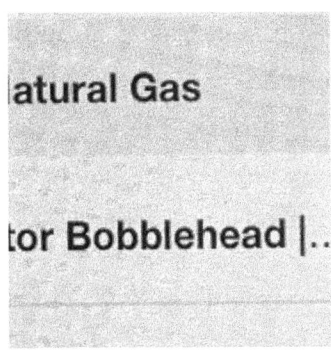

Bobblehead was my favorite name for Gus, and here it appeared on my screen just as I was thinking about him.

Until then, I hadn't thought much about reincarnation. I know my brother Call's spirit is with me and guides me, and he sends me signs, especially of comfort when I most need it, in nature. But I haven't sensed that he's returned as a person, and I haven't felt that way about other beings who've passed from my life.

I became intensely curious about the possibility of animal communication in the afterlife, and I hoped Gus would decide to come back in some form.

When my mind latches on to a question, I'm a diligent researcher. I happened upon the books of Karen A. Anderson, a respected animal communicator, whose book *The Amazing Afterlife of Animals* gave me hope. However, I learned she has retired from mediumship. Eventually, I found Sunny Mann, a practitioner who partnered with Karen to help her sanctuary through Sunny's work in animal communication, healing, and behavior correction. I engaged Sunny to open a conversation with Gus.

Sunny lives in Caroline Springs, Victoria, which is located in the countryside of Melbourne, Australia. We've never met. What follows are transcripts of our communications over a period of a year — unedited, for the most part.

Be amazed!

❧ 3 ❧
HOW TO READ THE TRANSCRIPTS

In the following pages, I include transcripts of sessions Sunny had with Gus, which she emailed to me. I saved these with the dates, and I present them in chronological order. You'll find the flow significant.

I include my journal entries, which I either dictate into my phone or type on my laptop. I dated my notes as the thoughts occurred, often when I was reading or rereading Sunny's session transcripts.

In her emails, Sunny also recorded visions that occurred to her during the sessions. We eventually realized that Gus was implanting these images (and sometimes sounds and feelings) in her mind. For example, he showed scenes of he and I being together, of family gatherings, and also of my hospitalizations before they occurred. But neither Sunny nor I could explain the meaning or the context of many of the scenes in her visions. It was only later I began to realize that among these impressions, Gus was conveying images of events from our past lives.

4
GUS IN THE AFTERLIFE

SESSION 1 – DECEMBER 12, 2023

Sunny reported, "This is Gus speaking":

Of course, Sunny, I was aware that you would talk to me soon. I am only just realizing what's happened to me and that I have moved to a different realm. Please tell my family that I am well. They won't be able to believe that.

How is it even possible that I am well without them?

But I am like a young dog again, running freely and enjoying the peace and calm of this place. I arrived here straightaway, even before my mom realized that I was gone. I hung around my family and particularly Mom for a while.

How could I just be cool without my body?

But once I saw this realm and reached here, the welcome, the warmth, and the love was all *divine!* I met some known souls and I am not alone here. Leaving behind the pain and suffering is nice.

No more of it now, Mom.

Please believe me when I say this that my time was finished. Everything is based on the soul contract. I had come for a short but intense life. It was about the quality and not the quantity. It was the life worth living — so profound, so meaningful, and so relished! It was meant to happen the way it did, Mom and Dad.

My mom is a superhuman, and her love is like a fragrance that travels far and wide. I was lucky to always be enveloped in it.

Sunny asked, "Are you coming back, Gus?"

Is that even a question? Of course I am coming back! It's maybe a year or two, maximum, before I return. How will I be found? It will all happen on its own because that's how everything will align. We will be together and this time for a very long time. I will make sure that Mom will be happy with the length of my life when I come back.

But why are you so lost, Mom? I'm still with you, but of course you can't feel my weight or touch me, nor do you have your brown shadow following you anymore. I was your Velcro baby! I was where you were, especially at home.

To depart is normal, and thus it happened. It also makes us understand the true worth of another being. I'm not saying that you didn't have that understanding for me, but it rubs in the fact that we dilly-dally, thinking there will be many tomorrows. We don't know when the last one is not a tomorrow, but just a today.

Where would you find another faithful servant soul? I adored and still adore you and continue to be with you. Your grief really doesn't have a meaning because souls never die, and Gus lives on.

When I come back, it will not be a new soul, but *me* in a different body. So there is no end — only a continuation. Oh, Mom! No, please don't shed any more tears as it hurts me beyond words. I want to see you enjoying life and having maximum love, fun, and joy. When I see you sad, I feel helpless because I find the grief has shadowed my presence with you. No more of grief! Christmas is just around the corner, and the show must continue.

I have so much to share, Sunny. My life was a bliss, and I enjoyed each and every minute of being with the family — the fun and frolic. I'm lucky that I could enjoy so very much, including my free runs — leash-free ones were my favorite. I was also all out to impress you with my loyalty and obedience.

I enjoyed all the things puppy when I was young. I was cute and adored. And I enjoyed being with you all. I was trying to find ways to keep you pleased and happy. Once I got the hang of it, I figured it out. I quickly understood how to conduct myself. Your words were my command. The closer I could be with you, the better I felt.

I was the son of the family. I came to a family who loved and cared for my life. The running and chasing was fun, and it was important to enjoy the outdoors. Fresh air and activities were my thing. I enjoyed the food I was given. It was rich and appropriate. I loved eating — so much I was sloppy!

I loved it when you chased me for things. I took part in fun activities because it bonded us well. I would do anything to be a part of my family's activities. I loved playing in water and with water.

Being on the couch and bed was the best time.

I loved winter months because of all the activities and the warmth generated.

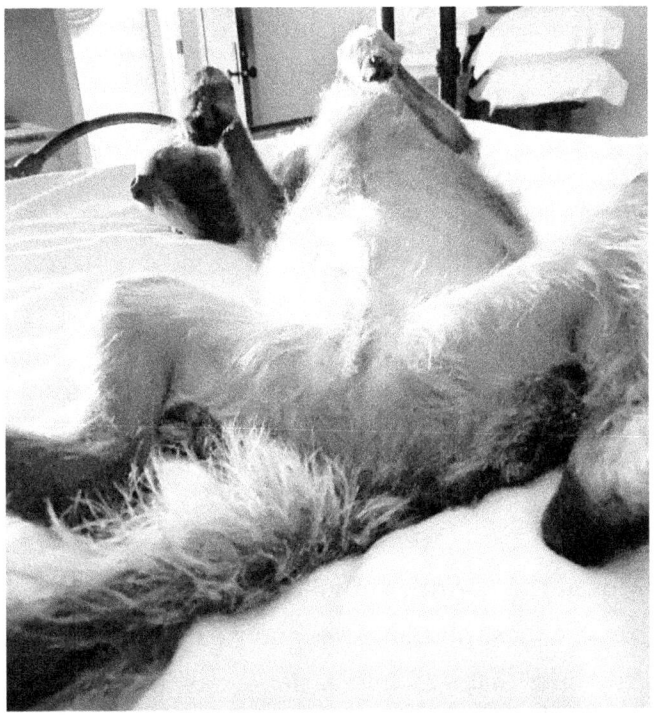

Sunny said Gus showed her his male organ. He posed and then slept this way often, and I suspected he knew he'd get a laugh.

I was my mom's child. I was her boy! I was very protective and possessive of her. I didn't care much about anything else. I was an easygoing one and had totally devoted my life to my mom. I would tell my mom the navigation strategies. It was important to work like a team.

The communication continued the next day. Sunny sensed Gus was feeling more settled.

When I was young, I was just a powerhouse of energy. I would play a lot, and later I would get exhausted and sleep. People loved me at all ages. I was kind and tolerant of most things. Even children were safe in my presence. Picking up things from nature to play with was my forte.

Sunny saw Gus picking up sticks.

I loved the warmth in the house, the heat source. I had the most pleading eyes and would beg for food. Anything that was human food was just too good to have missed. I loved the cold food that I could lick.

I became a very mature boy as I grew up. I was the loveliest boy in town. I was gentle and caring. Sometimes I was a sook too [Australian slang for *crybaby* or *wimp*]. I was a bit messy, swimming to reach the shore. I loved being curly and cuddly. I was full of life. I enjoyed being the center of attention and getting heaps of love.

I got super excited whenever I had to leave the house. Car rides with Mom and Dad were fun. I have enjoyed all my adventures. My family made an extra effort to take me to places where they thought we would have fun.

I was an integral part of the family and will always continue to be. I have gone *nowhere*, okay?

Sunny's Visions

> Gus is playing with a stuffed toy and shaking his head from side to side. He is galloping in water happily. He waits patiently and inquisitively, smelling the ground for something. He paws the air for attention with his front leg, barking happily and dancing. I see him excitedly spinning in circles. He gets belly rubs, rolling from side to side on his back. I see an open newspaper while Gus is on the floor looking up at it. As a puppy gingerly using the stairs, he is crawling up next to a big pot or vase.

I (Rebecca) note:

This is *so* true! When we were in the car together and he was in the back seat, he'd stand on the center console and stick his head out of the open sunroof. Then he kept pawing the air, and I couldn't figure out what he wanted. *Faster, Mom?* As for his spinning on the beach, people who were used to seeing him expected him to twirl on command! He brought them laughter and joy. Often he'd run around so much he'd end up in the ocean. And, yes, he'd scamper up the beach house stairs.

Gus said:

Mom and Dad, I am constantly with you. There's nothing that should change because I'm not there in the physical form. Your outdoor activities should continue the same way, Mom. You are the beacon of light that everyone needs.

Please do not let the light fade! Whenever you miss me, please just call me, and I will be there with you — which I am anyway! Please do not forget all the fun that we had playing together.

Sunny said, "I saw him playing tug with you."

You will see me in everything, and many dogs will remind you of me. I am very excited here. It is the growing grounds, and until I return, we will continue to meet like now. Take me to places even now. I am your forever baby and my connection with you is divine. We are made for each other, and mark my words, *I will return*, and will have double the enthusiasm. I will always stay your precious.

The same day, I (Rebecca) replied to Sunny via email:

Thank you, Sunny. Beautiful to wake up to see this message!

5
BEACH PARTY

SESSION 2 – DECEMBER 17, 2023

Sunny emailed the transcript of her second session with Gus. He told her:

I want to connect with Mom again. She is still so distraught. She still cries and rereads what I left for her. It hurts no end to see her like this. Can she please stay happy for me? She is my *sunshine*, and I can't see her so sad.

Sunny wrote, referring to me (Rebecca): Gus sensed you are planning a beach party. He said:

I love the thought of the beach party. Ask Mom to take lots of photos. I will be attending, for sure.

I noted:

After his passing, we had a celebration on the beach with my family and their dogs. We scattered his ashes in the ocean and some of it on the driftwood he would pee on.

Gus said:

I am so glad to have chosen you, Sunny. I tried bringing you back to my photo because I wanted to talk. I know that I spoke primarily about my mom the other day. I want to talk about all of them. The joy they have given me is unparalleled. My dad loves me a lot too. He has a lovely heart, and he holds a special place for me in his heart.

My friends miss me too, but they feel me around and it helps them a lot. I want you to continue doing the activities that you did when I was with you because I will join you all in them.

Mom, I keep sending messages and reminders. Please be slightly more alert. Your grief stops you from feeling it all. My *magic* lies in you; my *soul* is nestled in yours. We are *one!*

Now I'm more aware of my growth responsibilities here. It is a lovely, peaceful, warm, love-filled, and happy place. I really feel that I belong here.

The beauty of it is that I don't feel like being away on another realm but right here with you.

Mom, you're not far from me. We are living together still. The difference lies in the perspective, but souls can travel anywhere, including yours. You have visited me many times here as well. Some part of you feels relieved that I am healthy again, and the other part cries because I can't dance with you anymore.

Momma, I still can! I really can.

I just feel the need to tell you more that I am still *alive*. I'm really so. Don't let your brain and people tell you otherwise. They say so because that's all that is widespread and told. I can feel you whenever I want, and you can close your eyes and feel me too. I'm right here with you. Sit in silence and peace, and we can both meet whenever you want — anytime, anywhere, be it for the shortest of time or the longest. We will be as we always were. I have to teach you this because it will stop the unnecessary rolling down of tears. I can't sit on you with a thud and make you laugh anymore, but the peaceful connection will always remain.

What are you thinking of making for the party?

Gus showed Sunny something savory.

I think they will love it.

My shaggy looks made me such a superstar. I looked beautiful, the way I was. I couldn't give my adventures up for anything. That's what brought out the best in *me* — or, rather, *us!* Joy was in exploring the outdoors together. Being at home was calming too. The whole experience of being in a body brought so much joy and fun. Nothing could stop me from perusing anything if I put my heart and head to it.

I was a bad or good influence for a few souls — other dogs, friends, and family. I loved being the group leader and showing how things could be done differently. The beauty was in being given free rein to express myself. My family believed in me and my varied skills. My antics brought them so much laughter. I had my own peculiar ways of doing things. You might call them my quirks or strange attributes.

I noted to Sunny:

One of his dog pals was named Truman. When that dog would get rambunctious, Gus would bark to correct him, as if to say, "Calm down!" At other times, Truman would stand in front of Gus and bark constantly, but Gus wouldn't bark back. He'd sit down stoically and look up to me, as if telling me to get Truman to shut up.

Gus said:

If I didn't wet my legs, then I didn't achieve much. Boy! Did I care about the time of the day or the temperature? I just believed in living to the *fullest*. I really want my family to believe in the same.

Look at me! I had a short stint in a dog's body, but we all have a soul contract. Enjoy as much as you can, while you can. We all understand the gift of good health.

You already know all of this, Mom, and I am a living example of it. I *love* you with all my depth, and I will continue to be your protector. Everyone knows my love for my family and people. I will always be there.

I am so glad you understood what I was talking about the other day. I was prepared for my departure, and seeing the light wasn't difficult for me. I'm so glad I could tell you about myself almost immediately.

I am where you are!

Your love for music makes the house a home — it soothes all the souls living there. Carry it on and carry it forward. Please live life to the fullest. I really want you experiencing much more enjoyment than ever before. You are still very tender and it will *heal.* You are my *light* and my meaning of being. I said this before and I will tell this again. You are my priority. I will get busy here, but I can still be with you all the time as such is the power of being in light. Part of my energy will always be with you. The bed feels empty, doesn't it? I'm there every night watching over you all.

Sunny's Visions

> I hear an appliance noise, which I think is in a kitchen. I see two people embracing. The hold lingers. Gus waits on the front steps of the house; his patience is a kind of stillness. I see a woman's chest — a hand brushing something off it. There is sand piled up on something bumpy and noisy. It is an outdoor setting in the late evening, with someone seated in a comfortable chair in front of a firepit in a patio area. People sit, looking relaxed, seeing neighbors. A male hand takes a drink bottle from an ice chest. I catch the aroma of food floating in the air, a breeze

coming in. Gus loves staying warm indoors. Mom takes out a few food items and lays them on a bench. She is undecided about something to do with it. There is company in the kitchen, someone resting against the wall.

Gus continued, as if remarking on the scene:

You are my *darling* family! Here is my message: *Bring the joy back into the house!* You both bring *joy* to many. Mom, try to stay warm today.

As you are my *all*, I am your *all* too. Together we can continue to enjoy the hues. You are the gift I treasure. Mom, I am always going to be with you — body or no body!

From My Journal

December 31, 2023

Having read Sunny's transcript of this session, I wrote in my journal:

I decided to run down the Greenway [the path where I jog] because I couldn't bear to be in the house that long. We're back in Atlanta now. As I was running, this dog came running up to me, and I felt Gus's energy. Then I heard a hawk screaming in a tree. As I made the turn on the path, I saw a beautiful rainbow. It was so rare. I knew and felt Gus when I saw it.

Today I still feel some heaviness with Gus's loss. I decided to take a beach walk before we flew back, and I saw another couple who had lost their dog. I told them about Gus. Then I walked farther down, and I talked to Gus. I told him how much I missed him, how much joy he brought us, and how grateful I was for his being in our lives.

And I told him how much I hoped he would be back. Then it occurred to me that I would love to see an eagle. Then, at the end of the path where I usually turn around to return home, there was a beautiful bald eagle soaring above me. Then I saw a puppy with a ball in his mouth, and I was again reminded of playtime with Gus. When I was walking back, I looked out to sea and thought I would love to see some dolphins. Halfway back from my walk, several dolphins appeared out on the water.

I came to think of sightings of eagles and hawks as signs from Gus.

It was sad to leave our beach house because it feels as if I'm leaving a piece of him behind. But we will be back in February.

I love you, Gus.

Today's Dad's birthday, so maybe you will show up for him.

JANUARY 2, 2024

In my first entry of the year, I wrote in my journal:

Yesterday was New Year's, and as always, Gus, you are on my mind. Every morning I get up, have my coffee, and sit outside thinking of you. Dad joined me yesterday. When we were sitting out there, two red-tailed hawks circled each other in the sky above the woods. Both Dad and I felt your presence. Later that afternoon, we went walking on the golf course. I was listening to a podcast on predictions for the new year and how we can manifest our reality. As I was talking with you and asking you to come back, I spotted a tennis ball on the ground. Seeing your favorite toy warmed my heart, especially at that moment.

Later that day, I was sitting out on the lounge chair. As I lay there, I could've sworn I heard your little whine, like you would do when you wanted me to let you out of the house.

I love you, Gus, and I'm waiting for you to come back.

6
PLAYING IN BOTH WORLDS

SESSION 3 – JANUARY 3, 2024

In their session, Gus told Sunny:

I am wonderful, Sunny! I am enjoying both the worlds. I am constantly playing with my friends on Earth and also in this other realm. I have to be focused on my spiritual journey here, but the beauty is that I can be in parallel planes and do so many things at the same time. I can't just turn away and walk off when my love is here. I'm having abundant company.

Sunny asked him, "Were you trying to connect, Gus?"

Of course, my mommy needs me more than anyone does. No matter how hard she tries, she can't stop thinking of the amazing pact that we had and still have. Our lives shared purpose. My fun, my joy, my antics, my goofiness, my smartness, my alertness, my everything made her happy. My presence was what mattered to her. She could do and still does anything in the name of Gus. She is my *all*. Her heart is so pure, Sunny! I can't believe there are people like her. Others matter so much to her. She believes in making a big impact in everyone's life, be it other creatures or humans. She believes in being her best self in life.

Please tell Mom that all accounts are held here. All good deeds are rewarded by offering higher rungs, orbits. Mom, you are so *special*, and I am so proud you are my mom.

***Sunny said,* "You are amazing, Gus! You work out ways to make us understand that you want to connect."**

Sunny, I can't thank you enough. You have brought so much joy to all of us. We connect and communicate through you. I hope you do not mind.

"No, not at all, Gus. Your mom and family will be super happy to hear from you."

Sunny, does not being in a body and not being able to tap your legs while sitting matter?

"Yes and no, Gus. Yes, because your family and friends can't touch you physically because everyone was so used to seeing you, touching you, hugging you, playing with you, and feeding you. No, because now they can only sense you. They find it terrible that they are unable to touch you and feel you."

Is it terrible even if they can still feel me like in lucid dreams?

"That's right, Gus."

Is that why there is so much sadness and everyone feels sorry for me and Mom? But I'm here!

"Yes, Gus. Your mom and dad firmly believe you are there. Your mom told me she felt you at the beach party, and when she was walking on the beach, and at other times in the house."

Yes, I know. I can hear and understand it all. I remember there was this really happy, goofy dog on the beach. I soul-shared with that one for a while. If any dog shows interest in my mom, she should know it is me soul-sharing, and she can feel and hug me abundantly. I am forever with them and feel sad that they feel sad at my departure.

I am very much here. Mom needs to watch carefully because she will get further signs from me. She shouldn't worry she's trying to sense me in everything. Yes, I really want to hang out with her as before. No one should think she is crazy. I can't tell you how it hurts to see her somber and quiet.

Celebrate like there is no tomorrow! Live like we're all together.

Mom, I am very happy about a few things you are progressing with. With a sincere heart, you should carry on. I have heaps to talk about.

Sunny asked him, "What was your purpose in your mom's life?"

My purpose was to give *her* some purpose — to help her feel comfortable during her midlife crisis. She saw me as an opportunity to do some really cool things. Her involvement in life and her direction in life shifted with me there. Her quality of life was enhanced. She felt complete in a spiritual sense. Our longing for and dependence on each other only grew each day. We were and are a force to be reckoned with! My desires were like her command. I can say I thoroughly enjoyed it, and the others in our lives did as well.

I was never the insignificant one but always the "hero" of the show. I had a loud presence and, as you know, I still do. I kept the whole household coordinated and connected.

After my passing, there is a void in those left behind, but I'm always there in spirit to provide them solace and direction. They seem lost coming to grips with the situation. Please tell Mom that our purposes are connected. Just as she needs me, I needed her equally to flourish in life and to shine stronger.

My energies were high because my family gave me an opportunity to rise and be myself. I enjoyed all the attention and fame. I also played my role rather well. My happiness knew no bounds. Even when I rested, I had a certain joy and believed in myself. I never let my spirits down, even if other things were out of alignment.

I can never forget the fuss and attention I got toward the latter part of my life for my well-being, and during the early part of my life due to my cheekiness. I was a highly tuned-in pet, who had something to contribute toward every being I came to know. I was also very emotionally strong and faced adversities with a smile. I tried to be mature yet playful. I believe one can be responsible, yet be in the moment for total fun.

I want to say hello to Mom and to convey my feelings to her. I want her to understand the deeper me, the brainier and more logical me. Sometimes such traits can get lost in a cheerful personality.

"You are doing such clever things, Gus!"

I will want to be connected from time to time, as I am a newly transitioned soul. I feel the need to do it more now. When things settle and a new normal is developed, I will ease up because by then I will have helped my Mom with her healing.

"You can connect as often as you like, Gus. We would love for you to feel heard."

I still look in wonderment at the love for me. My parents' hearts are big, and to love so much is almost too beautiful to watch. Not a day goes by when I am not discussed in the household, and I enjoy listening to all the lovely things that are spoken about me. The fur friends feel happy and relaxed in my company. Mom also notices and experiences my mannerisms in the other pets. Let me say this purely: I want to stay and remain the most important baby forever. I want to stay alive in their warm hearts because I am still the same.

Sunny's Visions

Mom is avoiding the waves, jumping to prevent the water touching her feet. Someone is sitting on their knees and concentrating on someone else, who is calling, "Bec!" Gus tells me, "My mom is Bec," and she holds his leash in her hand. He is walking along the beach, sniffing the sand, jumping and running, startling the birds at the beach party. There is a long string of Christmas lights. Momma made the cake. She is telling the other dog to behave around the kitchen area. She's nervous, dusting something as she releases pent-up energy. She's on the phone — something pink or purple near her. She sniffs, making a kissing sound, takes deep breaths. Then she's on a hammock or something that would sway. She is very patient. She attracts others to herself due to her pure energy, just like a magnet.

Gus went on:

Mom commands attention without asking. Someone else is complaining of back pain and worries a lot. I think it's Dad. Mom doesn't need anything for herself. It is always for others.

Sunny, I want to talk so much more. We can always talk again if you feel exhausted though.

Sunny answered, "Let's talk some more now as I feel a little energized."

Okay! My dad is always thinking big stuff. He contemplates a lot, and it seems very stressful to me. He needs to relax and leave everything to the universe. I will sort out everything for them all. Dad appreciates my mom's involvement and also how she binds the family together. Dad likes it when he can enjoy his life as well, which I think he should do more often. My passing has been a wake-up call that life can't be taken for granted. Mom is a little fussy about getting everything right, but Dad goes with the flow when he's with Mom.

They enjoy social company, and I loved it too. It was so much fun. There was happiness in the air and laughter too. We looked forward to the energy from guests in the house because a household can get too serious when it's only us at home. During quieter times, I would curl up and lie down, but I always kept an eye on everything that was taking place.

I want to say to Mom: *Please do not change for anyone or anything.* You are perfect as you are. You underestimate your worth. You make a huge difference in everyone's life, including your own, even if you don't realize it. I love it when I see you happy. Then I can enjoy your feelings with you. But if you get sad, then I have no other choice but to feel the same sadness. Even now, I still feel you and your energy. I am really happy that you have come a long way since my departure. One thing is for sure: In happiness, we can both rejoice.

Traditions should carry on and should be made stronger. Mom, I can read you like an open book even now, just as I could read your thoughts when I was in my body. The joy of life is in getting out and about. The freshness, the chill, the thoughts, and the love nourish the health that helps us stay alive. You are stronger than the strongest. Belief in self and in others makes you strong because we get strength from each other's energy.

You are surrounded by the best. Your Gus is with you every step of your journey.

Do you eat meat, Sunny?

"Yes."

Oh! My mom is very particular [about what she allows herself to eat].

"Okay, I will ask her, Gus baby."

I am my mamma's baby.

"Are you upset I called you 'baby'?"

No! But it is my momma's prerogative to call me thus. But I am very grateful to you, Sunny, for everything.

"Gus, I love you equally for it. Thank you, Gus darling."

That's better. Can I talk you again, Sunny?

"Yes, of course, Gus!"

From My Journal

JANUARY 3, 2024

I wrote:

I woke up and saw a text message from Sunny on my phone. I was reading it, then I put it down. When I came back to it and was looking at my emails, her text and my text showed up in my emails. That has never happened to me before. I figured that was Gus trying to talk to me. I put my phone down because I had to take a minute to make sure what I saw was real. When I picked my phone up again, I noticed the emails were no longer there, but were back as texts. I reached out to Sunny and told her. She said Gus obviously has more to talk about. When I returned to looking at my emails, one of the subject lines was "Bobblehead," which is what we used to call you. Dad and I were just talking about you prior to me looking at my emails. Then I went down to the river to run and saw a kestrel, which sat on a log until I finished running, then drove back home. I know you guide me and you're there with me.

January 4, 2024

I woke up early and went outside, as I always do, to meditate. I was thinking of you and saw a hawk in the tree. It looked like another kestrel. I felt you there. I have another session with Sunny at 5:30 today because she said there's more you want to talk about, which is so funny because you always were so talkative and we loved it. Now we have someone who can communicate with you and translate.

January 6, 2024

On my first day of my shamanic initiation, I felt your energy, Gus.

This ñusta prepares the tools she will use in a shamanic ceremony.

That night, I was lying in bed, thinking about my ñusta initiation with the master shaman, Don Alejandro. [Ñustas represent many aspects of Pachamama (spirits of the native land) and the Universe. All women are ñustas.]

I felt and heard a loud scratching as if you were pawing the ground, Gus. It woke me up. Then I felt a soft nudge around my ankle, and I felt you touching me. It was such a warm feeling.

JANUARY 7, 2024

I saw a hawk when I was outside, meditating and thinking of you, feeling your energy. I read what Sunny said and it brought tears to my eyes because it was so beautiful. I know you're coming back. I just feel it.

JANUARY 8, 2024

Today is my daughter Lauren's birthday. There's something in the air that feels light. I saw a beautiful peregrine falcon down at the river.

I was thinking of you again, Gus, while walking down the river, when all of a sudden, a hawk flew out of the woods at eye level, about twenty-five feet in front of me. The bird flew over the fence and landed on the ground. It had something in its mouth. I feel your presence every time I go to the river. In one of the messages, you said to Sunny I was your *sunshine*. Tonight I heard a song about sunshine and the lyrics mentioned the month of May. I had another session with a different pet communicator and she said you said you will be back. This made me so happy. Plus, Sunny said the same thing. The song that came on tonight that mentioned the month of May as one of the lyrics made me think you're telling me you'll be back in May. Time will tell.

January 10, 2024

You were very quiet today. I did not see any signs from you, but I did contact Sunny. I asked her to let me know if you had anything to say about my surgery on January 12. I kept feeling I was going to have a near-death experience and see you. I was feeling very uncomfortable. Sunny felt the same thing on January 10, because when she texted me, she gently insinuated something magical would happen, but I did not connect the dots until last night. I told her what I was feeling, and she said, "Oh wow, Rebecca! I just got goosebumps because Gus unexpectedly showed up on my notepad twice." She asked about the surgery and said she was not trying to be intrusive or invasive. I told her about it and also reminded me of what she saw in one of the readings in December — a woman standing naked, a hand over her two breasts.

7
MY HEALTH CHALLENGE

SESSION 4 – JANUARY 10, 2024 (BEFORE MY SURGERY ON JANUARY 12, 2024)

I had known for some time that I needed surgery. I was worried about it. Of course, Gus was worried too. Here's how he helped me through it.

Sunny said, "Hi, Gus. Do you want to connect?"

Yes, yes, yes, yes! Why else would I send you the message in doubles?

"How are you, Gus?"

I'm good, Sunny! I love this new energy around my mom. She will flourish in it. I was on this journey of hers, and I am always just next to her.

"Do you think your mom is in isolation?"

Not at all. How can she be alone when I am with her all the time? Ask Mom not to be fickle-minded: Her decision should be final. There is no good or bad in her situation or this instance. I will be with her irrespective of whatever she chooses. She is feeling overwhelmed because now she is more aware about how the body works, and it is as sacred as the soul that resides in it. You should treat it with utmost respect and care. This body provides the soul the identity, which you are known by. Whenever the awareness rises in you is the perfect time because you had to experience something to develop the appreciation. Relax and leave the rest to the *cosmos*. You are a valued member of the cosmos, and I am your forever companion. Both of us together will make our existence profound and exceptional — more like *magical*, Momma.

> Sunny saw Gus nudging me and shaking me with his front legs.

Gus advised me:

Drop all your fears and anxiety about everything in life. There is no need for it because you are complete in yourself. Your solitude is a beautiful reminder of the power that resides within you. You tap into it with purity and honor, with gratitude, and you will be amazed.

Just as you believe in others, please believe in yourself with the same intensity. You have been purified on numerous occasions to become the *new you*. Whatever you make of it is for you to decide because I can see this huge energy bubble enveloping you, which is your protection layer. Your calling is here.

You can take it to another level if you want — because, even if you touch one person, you have attained divine powers. People in medicine and naturalists have an element of this in themselves, some of the God-cosmos energy.

You will be in good hands forever. Your Gus is also your shield, and you know it and feel it.

I can understand the weird feeling you're experiencing and the challenges of the conditioning of your brain, but you can set your *new* norms and live by them. You do not have to fit in a circle. You would benefit by gravitating toward your heart rather than an appearance that has to be put up for display. This doesn't mean that you become a recluse. It means that you can be with all beings and things, yet by yourself. You do not have to be removed from any setting, but people who come in your contact will automatically benefit because of your radiating energy.

Sunny saw me holding somebody's hand.

Gus described this vision:

Your touch will act like a transfusion of good energy in the other person. Your shield bubble always needs to be maintained such that you can make it a one-way energy release. Your energy needs will always be replenished.

You will enjoy being the *new you* — the centered and grounded you. You are the *light* that is needed by the ones around you. You won't have to make any effort for it. Your energy can be purified on a full-moon night on the beach as well as by using the sun energy on the beach. If and where possible, stand or sit in the water for the energy exchange to be stronger. But keep safety in mind as you may go much deeper than you may think you would. Getting a companion to keep a watch on you would be a great idea.

Leave the things of nature alone. They have a purpose there, so you should respect and believe in that. The whole cosmos is designed to serve us, and each component stands where it belongs.

The energy center and energy sources are scattered all around us. We — those who are tuned in to the energy — will find it anywhere and everywhere. Even a glass of pure water is an energy source, where the energy is topped up.

Your soul has started to wander, which is fine, but keep your protection at the highest levels. You will be visiting arenas that very few have touched or approached. None of this feels strange to you because you have known this before. Just as we have always belonged together, this knowledge has also always stayed with you. Each stage of life is based on what you have intended in your soul contract. Each phase has a great purpose.

Nothing bad exists uselessly either. All good and bad experiences occur to teach you things you were and are meant to be introduced to. The power bursts happen based on how much can be channeled quickly by you. Too much can be dangerous and impossible to handle, thus a balance is maintained and managed for you so that the extra energy may not harm you.

You may surrender to whomever you want to believe in, and they will channel you to intensities appropriate at different stages.

Momma, this feels like a strong connection. We will both be able to understand it at a deeper level. The future holds excitement for both the heart and the soul. The fluttering feeling you have happens because the exposure is too sensational. Your awakening is different from most people of your race. Your past lives have a real contribution toward it. You were connected and grounded deeply in one of them. Your association with the earth is very strong, but so is the connection with sky and water. Most of the elements will complete you.

You are on the path of self-actualization, for you will be blown away with all that will come into your path. But you must pace yourself to be better able to transcend these experiences and transfer the energy.

Mom, I can speak to you at a different level now. You will benefit and grow from everything and everyone that crosses your path. Listen to people intently and carefully. They will have messages for you. You will get the messages midsentence, and only you will know that the message is intended for you. The logical brain has no role in any of this because you will only operate from the space of total *love*.

Don't let any of this scare you, but this is where you are headed. I will be your guiding light, along with the other sources. At no time will I make you feel alone. I truly love you at all levels of awareness. We are bonded, and that is the most precious feeling we have for each other.

Understand that I was your guru and guiding soul in your previous birth.

Sunny's Visions

> I feel an energetic hand on someone who is lying straight on their back. I see a black cat licking someone's face. Sheep or cattle are being rounded up by another animal, maybe a dog. I feel the vertigo of a whirlpool. I see blue sky with a few scattered clouds. There is someone at an elevated level — a much higher level than the ground. I see legs dangling in water, struggling to open a gate, lots of steps leading to something like an ancient temple, which is on a height. A shaman tribe is sitting around the same scene (much like the photos you sent of your shamanic initiation). I see something boiling

on an earthen stove (some traditional practice) in a mud hut. Someone is sleeping in the bed while the other occupant leaves the bed as covers are pushed back. (This happens today or in the future.) Now I see a two-story building (in the present time), which looks like a hospital. I see a wheelchair, an emergency exit, and an electronic entrance. Dug-up ground is narrow and dark, as if construction is going on. A person is lying in bed in the hospital, their body being dragged. The legs have no sensation, resting in bed. A pet jumps up to join the person on the bed. I see what looks like golf clubs or sticks in a container or vase. There is a ceremony or activity involving sprinkling or putting something on a person. The person is surrounded by two or three people, including a man in bright silk. A duvet in peacock colors covers a woman's body (in some ancient time). In the present or future, I see something scanned or magnified by a phone — the image of someone lying in the bed and staring at the ceiling.

Sunny told Gus, "Tell something to Mom so that she knows it is you."

Gus replied:

Do that something to your hair!

Sunny asked him, "Should Mom be scared for the surgery?"

No, not at all! Keep the protection on!

From My Journal

January 11, 2024

I wrote:

Today is the day before my surgery. I feel better about it. It's a beautiful day. I sat outside as I always do, meditating, and I saw a beautiful peregrine falcon up in the tree sunning itself. It made me smile. When I get up in the morning, I watch the sunrise. I want to feel the sun on my face. I felt Gus and I were showing our faces to the sun together.

Later this morning, I was by the river and saw another hawk, then I saw a beautiful blue heron leaping out of the water. I still feel good about the surgery. I will allow and trust.

When I intended to finish my four-mile walk today, something told me to just keep going and do one more mile. As I was getting ready to turn around, I happened to look up, and there was yet another hawk — right there on the limb. It was the first one I saw during my walk, and it was preening itself, which I took as a confirmation that my breasts are going to be healed and the operation will go well.

Tonight Gus was really on my mind as I was taking my shower. I remembered being with him at the vet's emergency room. I stayed by his side for four hours. Jim came and stayed with Gus too. We got to feel him and talk to him the entire time. I kept thinking of his face as they rolled him back to surgery. He was looking at me and seemed confused. I told him I loved him, which was the last time.

I could not help but think about my surgery, when I will be on the gurney being rolled into the operating room. I got really sad because of the vision of Gus being rolled in. I had music on after my shower, and "Over the Rainbow" came on. I started to cry thinking of Gus and the picture I took of him on the beach with a rainbow behind him. I felt his presence so much through this song and felt he was communicating to me.

We are a team with the rainbow because rainbows would show up on the beach when we were together walking, Gus chasing the birds.

How I miss him!

I underwent surgery as planned on January 12, 2024. I made no notes that day.

January 13, 2024

I'm feeling very good tonight, the day after my surgery. It is Friday the thirteenth! I definitely overdid it today. Stella [Kim's dog and Gus's great love] is here with us. We walked all around the backyard and went to the store with Jim. I did too much walking, and I moved my arms more than the doctor had advised. Throughout the day, I noticed two red-tailed hawks at the house, sometimes flying, and other times perched in the trees. I thought it was very strange because I have never seen them stay as long as they did today.

Tonight when Jim was helping me with post-op treatment, I felt a clot in my left breast and started feeling nauseous. I was shaky and had to go to the bathroom. As Jim was helping me walk, I fainted on the floor of the bathroom. Moments later, I regained consciousness and heard Jim calling my name. I know it scared the hell out of him because he thought I had died.

Two passengers - looking not so much bored as thoughtful, perhaps even worried.

Jim drove me to the hospital, where I learned I had a hematoma and would have to undergo surgery a second time, but not tonight. I was able to come home.

I had no pain. I stayed outside a good bit of the day to get some sunshine. It felt so good!

I thought of Gus a good bit, missing him so much today. In the days right after Gus's passing, I did a lot of running around out of the house on errands and such. Those activities were a distraction. Now, because I am recuperating,

Whenever Stella stayed with us, these two were never apart.

I need to stay home, and I find it's difficult getting used to the feeling that Gus isn't here with me.

Tonight I felt him strongly when I walked into the shower. I smiled and thought of Gus doing the "walk of shame" as we used to lead him into the shower for his bath. But once he felt the water on him, he was such a good boy, letting Dad and me wash him up! When he was clean, he would always feel much better and more energized. After my shower, I again had music playing, and the song "Over the Rainbow" came on again, then "Count on Me."

Call on me! I will be there! I knew it was him giving me a message that he was with me. I can talk to him, and I know he will be back because we have work to do together with the rainbow energy.

Now that I've written this, I feel at peace and very settled being at home today.

I love you, Gus!

JANUARY 15, 2024

I woke up thinking of Gus. Last night I started reading the book, *The Pet I Can't Forget* by Karen A. Anderson. It really helped me understand my grief as well as how Gus is communicating with me.

As I do every morning, I went outside with my coffee to meditate and watch the animal kingdom wake up. Of course, my first priority was to see if there was a sign from Gus. Usually a huge hawk appears in a tall tree. The bird loves to bask in the early morning sun. When I see this hawk, I feel it is Gus. We sit outside [as we did when he was with me in body] soaking up the morning rays. But this morning, the hawk was nowhere to be seen when I sat down, so I made a wish for Gus to show me a sign through the hawk. When I looked up, there was the hawk flying to his limb. It brought joy and a smile to my face.

Around ten in the morning, I found a podcast with Karen Anderson being interviewed about pets after they die. I listened to it as I was walking inside the backyard fence.

I stopped walking, hoping I would get a sign.

All of a sudden, this tiny bird flew right up to me, then rose high in the sky. It was very apparent Gus was letting me know he was near!

Today was the second day we had Stella stay with us because Kim was traveling. Poor Stella! Last night when she came into the house, she was looking for

Gus and howling. She still seemed confused when she woke up today, but having her here is bringing me a lot of comfort. Two huge owls have hung around the house all day. Their presence makes me think Gus's energy is with us. Then when Stella and I were walking around the corner in the back, there was a bright-red cardinal sitting in the tree. I know Stella is sensing Gus because she now seems so attached to me wherever I go. I am so glad she is here with me to give me comfort. Her loving spirit helps me sense Gus is present with us.

JANUARY 16, 2024

Two red-tailed hawks have been staying around the house since my surgery. I feel Gus's energy through them. I love knowing he is close to me.

JANUARY 17, 2024

I went back to the doctor today because of the hematoma. I realized that Sunny's vision of hospitals and dragging of legs was about me. Gus was saying I'd be in and out and then back in the hospital. It was definitely a hard lesson to learn, but I'd had no idea I was overdoing it like I did.

Surgery took only an hour and I was able to come home this afternoon. Lauren had already planned to be here for me and to look after Stella. Both of them have been taking great care of me. I am definitely resting so much more.

I looked at my phone earlier and saw Sunny had reached out to me, wondering how I was doing. I told her what had happened. She said she felt a strong need to reach out to me, but she wasn't sure whether I felt connected to Gus after reading her emails to me.

JANUARY 18, 2024

I was sitting outside this afternoon and talking to my friend Annie about Lauren's pregnancy. Just then I saw one hawk fly vertically — no, horizontally — right across my field of vision, as though trying to get my attention and give me a message. Then I saw another hawk come and go. Then another that landed on the limb close by. All three were definitely making their presence known to me.

JANUARY 19, 2024

I woke up and heard a dog walking in our bedroom. The door was closed, and Lauren and I were in bed. I felt it was Gus's presence.

I had a class with Don Alejandro Apaza's shaman daughter. It is on ñusta healing, which relates to the rainbow. Just before the class, a red-tailed hawk flew onto a limb directly in my line of sight. I knew it was a message from Gus. He was saying, *You are on the right track because we are going to work together on the rainbow energy.*

JANUARY 22, 2024

This morning, Jim and I sat out on the lounge where Gus always sat with us while we drank our coffee. I was reading a book, and out of the corner of my eye, I saw two ghostlike blurs float by and disappear. I felt it was a sign Gus was with us. There were a lot of crows around as well, an unusual sight.

Today, I'm really feeling Gus's energy, and I miss him a lot.

Right after I saw those ghost images, I was looking at Zsófi's [the breeder's] Facebook page, where I saw a photo of two puppies that were available. One of them was labeled "The Boy," which is what we often called Gus. Somehow I sensed those two blurs I saw were the spirits of those Vizsla puppies.

This is the week was when Jim and I had told Zsófi we would pick one of the puppies from the mating of her dogs Hara and Extreme. [But we made no decision just then.]

We will see how everything works out.

8
SELF-HEALING

SESSION 5 – JANUARY 25, 2024

Gus said to Sunny:

Hi, Sunny! Next time, please just listen to me when I ask for you. I really had to make my mom know I wanted to communicate with you.

***Sunny replied to him,* "It is all clear between us, Gus. Next time, I promise I won't put you through this."**

Please tell Mom she needs to stop the next step. It is totally unnecessary. She just doesn't need to go through it. Thank you for communicating my message to Mom. It is really important she heals totally before she goes for the next step.

"Do you mean the big scanning thing?"

[I had told Sunny I was planning to have an MRI after my surgery. My doctor thought it might be too soon, but I'd fretted about it and wondered whether it would ease my mind about healing.]

Gus had a strong opinion about the scan:

At this stage, it will lead to complications and would delay the healing. My mom needs to try doing self-healing as well. Can you guide my mom?

Sunny replied, "Of course I can do that."

Sunny, everyone has the power to self-heal, including the animals. It is primarily around believing in it and focusing on it.

You are a blessing in our lives, Sunny! What would I do without you? You understand me completely and even believe in me. You are meant for this work, and there's no doubt as to why Shubhi [Sunny's dog] is always raving about her mom. She is such a fine soul, and Sultan [her cockatiel] is so innocent and pure. His purity is of another level. I have enjoyed being with them.

Mom needs to understand that her body needs real food to heal faster. I wish she included everything in her diet that will help her to heal faster. It may seem like a simple procedure, but with age, healing of the body slows down, and the extra support of a nutritionist is needed to bring it back to a healthy level. Mom needs to look after herself for others — and, of course, for herself.

She needs to go on this amazing journey of finding herself [meaning my shamanic work], and it is only possible in a sound body. Please ask Mom to think about me and my advice: *Anything foreign or unnatural in the body only causes issues, which become difficult to cure.* Everything in moderation, even the best of food items. She is super blessed because of who she is. Mom is a valued member of the cosmos, and it starts at home. You only get back what you send out, just like a boomerang that always comes back to the sender.

Mom, you are feeling a little muddled and insecure or doubtful. Doubts are arising about a lot of things. Get into the peaceful zone, and you will be able to handle it all. Do you need someone to practice it on? Do you need Sunny to try and explore your gifts? I'm sure Sunny wouldn't mind any of this. The only thing needed is a detachment from everything that consumes your energy — be it people, gadgets, or thoughts. You are on the path of taking flight, but the longer you pause, the longer it will take you to gather momentum.

You can talk openly about any self-doubt or inhibitions. Never wait for the right time, as now is the right time and the perfect time. I'm waiting to be accompanying you on this. I am with you together now from this realm, and then later on, in a physical form. The momentum or the powerful push I give you from here will not be possible from me when I am once again in a body.

You know you are at a stage in your life when whatever you desire can be attained. I am not talking about materialistic things because they have no meaning in my eyes.

Please prepare yourself from the time you receive this message! We don't have time to waste.

You and many others will be on a special journey. It will make this lifetime worthwhile. Some people live for themselves, but life is really worth living for others.

How are the other important things going? You need to remove yourself from any stress about anything at all. As I said earlier, you need detachment. You cannot take the stress of others as your own. It won't make you a selfish person, but a *complete* person — someone who cares about serving others without being totally consumed in their issues. Each one of us is set out on our own journeys.

It is important to completely *fill* your oxygen tank before you lend the oxygen to others. Please let them flourish. Step aside — not to abandon them, but more to give them support from behind. Everyone you know, make them self-reliant. Those who need too much of your energy must be told once — and once only — the path to choose, then given the freedom either to follow or to make their own path.

I will always remember our physical time together, but I also remember that my state of health was consuming for you and caused you worry. This fact of life can never be forgotten. That is *death* — shedding the body. We all have a contract, and we have chosen what we want. There is no scope of error here from the *Boss*, the supreme. You know it well that the thought of death is scarier than the actual moment, and life starts to normalize again. I'm not trying to scare you about it or say that's where you're headed now — most definitely not. I want to relieve you of the fear, along with the emotional drain and lowering of vibration. We fear for others because our love creates attachment to them. But if you release this fear, you will be ready to live a truthful life, as seen from where I am. I assure you it is not your role to worry about someone else. You may think it is impossible, but knowing the reason behind what I say, you will gain wisdom.

All fears in your life are unfounded. Set yourself free by breaking all the shackles that create blockages. You know and have experienced so much in life, but now you have to begin with a clean slate. It doesn't mean sitting on a mountaintop to get in the present moment. It means being with all yet with *none*. Remove issues that suck up your energy and enthusiasm. I can understand that emotions can spill everywhere because of unsettled bodily issues, but simply build yourself up little by little, one by one.

Your Gus is by your side and will be with you all along.

I'm super excited being your boy! I had the best of everything then, and also now. You have to be an angel for all four-legged and two-legged beings. All the fur babies that you know, they can feel that special energy of yours, and so do the people around you.

Please unpack the reason behind what I'm saying. The whole family is worried for your well-being, but they need to remember that Gus is with you, and all will be set right, Momma. You can do the activities with other pets that you did with me. They will feel significant too.

Remember, I am always right next to you.

Mom, you told Sunny and Dad that you did not meet me in the hospital. Where were you expecting me? I was with you all the time, supporting you. You were protected by a layer of safety. There were many in attendance with you, including an older woman, someone you have a close affinity with. We were both waiting for you to recover from the anesthesia.

It was a day of revelation. What have you thought about or understood after that day? You are correct in thinking about everything you believe it to be, but thinking about it should not tie you down. I am forever moving beds with you! I like it and it doesn't bother me at all.

Sunny's Visions

> I see a woman lying straight, opened packaging material, and a few people gathered

around the fire, the sparks flying around. Gus licks something sweet with a long stroke of his tongue. I see a moving skateboard, which is later stationary. People are on a rooftop. I sense there is increased pulsation around the throat area. I hear Gus say he is Mom's boy. I see hills in the backdrop and someone tilling the earth surrounded by the brown stubble of crops.

Sunny asked, "Gus, who is tilling the earth?"

Gus replied:

My mom.

Continuing Sunny's Visions

Two men are sitting and smoking. Someone is walking fast at dusk. Gus is off leash, his body moving from side to side as he tries to walk very fast and not run. A lady is on the bed, unconscious, with her legs awkwardly bent. Someone says health is important. A woman tries to stand up with a sheet wrapped around her body. I see a smoke ceremony around a female body lying straight on the bed, either sick or lifeless.

Gus said to her:

Momma always left her physical body by being very sick in all her lifetimes, but she lived to an old age.

Continuing Sunny's Visions

I see the operating room with surgical instruments. Two nurses are preparing for the procedure. I see a mountain with trees and clouds meeting the trees. Two human babies sit dressed in cute old-fashioned clothing. An old lady tries to climb the steps of a house, but on her knees. Tomatoes and other vegetables are growing on the right-hand side of the path she is climbing. I see a small room, and a lady in light-green trousers and top is standing calmly in a dark corner. Another person runs out of there in a panic. Someone is hanging a sheet on a clothesline as seen in a photo. In the photo album, someone holds a framed picture of a toddler. A couple sits together in a bed, the male partner feeling the back of the other person's head. I see an antique pram with a woman in a bathrobe. A lady and a dog are standing at the top of a valley looking down at rocks and soil on the slope. Velvet curtains in a deep shade of red are being pulled aside.

Gus said:

I like to talk and not show as much. Mom is becoming aware of her surroundings. I want to be in my bodily form for my mom's journey. She takes each word of what I communicate to you with sincerity and thinks about it. That is where both of us feel connected because she laughs and loves solving the puzzle presented by the communication.

I can let you rest, Sunny. You need to look after your body too. My mom will be fine eventually, but for now it is time for introspection. My memory is very sharp, and I haven't forgotten anything at all. All that I care about is passing on my *love*. Me being myself and you being yourself can actually help a lot.

Continuing Sunny's Visions

> Gus relaxes, stretched out on an elevated space where there is food and a hot beverage. He walks toward the end of the back patio. The bushy tail of an animal looks like a stalk with leaves or petals on both

sides. Gus takes my attention from the top to the bottom, going from one leaf or petal down to the next. I see marshy land with puddles of water all around due to depressions in the ground. You cover yourself with a shawl as you look at the horizon. You are watching the sunset and the colored sky while sitting on a chair in the L-shaped corner of the patio. Gus hears your laughter as you say, "There is so much to tell Sunny!" Gus rubs against his dad's chin and feels the stubble. A lady comes down the stairs holding the railing as she carries a tray of four cupcakes or eggs. Someone sits on the floor with their back against the bed or sofa. You and Gus jump happily as you walk outdoors. You make space for Gus and call him to jump up and join you on the bed.

Gus said:

Ease up, Mom! You are more important than anything else. You don't fully understand your worth. You think you are a random or an ordinary person, but you are not. You are a revolutionary in many ways. Just believe in yourself. What is it that you are really wanting? Go all out! Give your all and nothing short of a hundred percent. Let's do it! You are the fragrance of love. Spread it far and wide!

Sunny asked Gus, "Should Mom worry about her health or anyone else's health in the family?"

Gus replied:

Not worried, but careful. Every action will have an effect. Go easy, yet cautiously. Being ill is a part of life, and she had health issues in all her previous lives too.

"Will Mom come out of it?"

Of course!

Gus ended the session by saying:

I need to appreciate my mom for all she does. The music, the smile — I know it all. Keep smiling and spreading the warmth. Your role is only to distribute love. Rest is not for you to worry about.

January 25, 2024

I emailed Sunny:

I did cancel the MRI. I told my family and the doctor I needed to let my body rest. Thanks for the advice, Gus and Sunny. Yes, of course, Gus. I believe nature with all of the elements are great healing tools, but sometimes that is not enough, so we may need help by using other healing modalities, such as reaching out to Sunny.

Yes, Gus. I needed to add real food gradually to my body — lots of protein, such as fish and vegetables. Gus, you know our broccoli routine! I was thinking that both of us had a similar situation when we were hospitalized. You had a massive bleed-out and I had a hematoma that bled out, but I survived. I have always been very healthy with high energy. This was one reason we bonded so well. We were always up for an adventure — until your passing.

Remember when we would go outside together in the early morning, then I would be still? We would watch sunrises and sunsets together at our beach home. You are and always will be my guidepost and copilot. We navigate this journey together.

Right now, I am taking steps toward our work I do envision you back with me. Together we are going to heal and support humans, animals, trees — everything related to nature. I understand this whole situation that has occurred to both of us. We gain more knowledge in other dimensions at a deep, profound level in our souls. It is a knowing within.

In the past, I have had premonitions that have come true. If I feel strongly in my gut to react, I will. If something happened and I hadn't reacted, I could never forgive myself. I was always a caretaker growing up, and I am making great strides to stay in my own lane.

Yes, of course, I would be concerned for your health and allergies. [Gus had allergies that had to be treated.] I would not have been a good dog guardian if I had ignored it. We finally got your body off the ear medication as well as all other medications. This was when you really thrived, and it brought you and us great joy to see you happy and thriving!

I understand there is a contract between us. Gus, I understand what you are saying, but I believe in healthy worry! I hope you understand.

Thank you. I love you, Gus. I know you are always with me, as you are right now while I am typing this. Both Sunny and I felt I was going to have a near-death experience, and I hoped I would see you. Thank you for protecting me while I was under [anesthesia].

Perhaps the older woman was my mother or grandmother. I love this, and it's so true!

Yes, Sunny, you do need to rest. This came to me very strong Wednesday night.

Here's Gus in a wistful moment at the beach house.

Yes, this is the description of the marsh and chair both Gus and I would sit in looking over the marsh, watching sunsets. It was so beautiful.

Ah, Gus, I have thoroughly enjoyed reading this for the second time. I am so grateful for your wisdom and protectiveness. We are blessed to have Sunny. Otherwise, I would not be able to read what you two talked about. Again, you are my guidepost and copilot.

I am learning a lot down here on Earth. We will be together soon, when the time is right, my boy! In the meantime, I know you are walking beside me. Your spirit is always with me when I talk to you — wherever I go. Big love, my dear Gus!

From My Journal

January 29, 2024

I wrote:

I was looking at photos of Vizslas online this morning. I told Gus how I love how he communicates with me, and I asked him to keep doing it. I ran errands to the supermarket and the furniture store, pretending he was with me bodily in the car. When

I went into the store, I left him in the car and assured him I'd be back. When I came back, I looked at my phone and saw this text message, which I took to be from Gus: *"I'm just trying, babe."*

I started laughing and was so stunned but happy! Right after Gus passed, I remember listening to the song "Heard Right" by Moth, which wails, "Got to be close to you."

I told Gus I love how he is communicating — and not to stop!

Later, I looked at my emails, and there was an article from *National Geographic* about how your dog can help you relax more than your human friends do. Then I read an article by Judith Newman, who found a way to help and understand autism with her son Gus!

I took it as a sign. *Let's keep communicating, Gus!*

JANUARY 31, 2024

This morning at 8:21 a.m., I was texting with Kim, and the word *Please* came up. I hadn't typed it and, looking at the thread, neither had she!

It was a new word from Gus!

Then another text came up on my phone:

"I'm just trying babe," with laughing and hug emojis!

This was the same message I got out of the blue last week! I knew then Gus was trying to reach out, but I decided to wait until the next session to tell Sunny because I did not want to bother her.

FEBRUARY 1, 2024

I wanted to reach out to Sunny because I felt a strong need from Gus's energy. I kept going back and forth debating whether to contact her. I was also feeling unsettled by not letting Sunny know. Finally, in the evening [my time] today, I did. Once I did, I felt better.

I talked to Gus when I was in the bathroom. I told him I would protect him and knew he wanted me to reach out. Then Jim and I were in the kitchen, and I said I needed to go back into the bathroom. I always play music in the evening, hoping our song "Over The Rainbow" comes on. It was playing as soon as I walked into the bathroom. I felt this was definitely confirmation Gus had heard me.

Sunny replied that she had promised Gus she would talk to him, but she hadn't yet. I assume she is very busy! She said she would do it soon. I told her no worries, that I was just curious if she had heard from him since I heard from him twice.

F℮bruary 2, 2024

Sunny wrote to me today and said Gus woke her up multiple times to tell me about the communication. She has finished the reading and recorded her visions. She said he is very keen that I spend the majority of my time developing my skills because my practice needs a lot of work still. She urged me to prioritize, saying it is more important than the current pattern of leading my life.

She will speak to me in a day or two.

I was taken aback because I was not sure whether Gus's referring to my skills was about my training with the Peruvian shamans.

I will soon find out!

❧ 9 ☙
JOY AROUND THE FIREPIT

SESSION 6 – FEBRUARY 2, 2024

In this session, the conversation goes three ways. Sunny emailed me the transcript of her conversation with Gus, as usual. Then as I read it over later, I inserted my questions and comments, only to keep reading and find that Gus had answered them in the session!

The firepit at home is a cozy place where our family often gathers. So it didn't surprise me at all when **Gus said to Sunny:**

The firepit that I talk about will be the place where Mom will reconnect with her real, experienced, and learned self.

Sunny said: **"When I invited Shubhi {my girl dog} to come to the session, she told me Gus is a higher-level guru soul, and she is learning a lot from him. Gus, I'm sorry I couldn't connect earlier."**

Yes, if you want to connect with me, it has to be done immediately. Understand that all the work I am doing here has to be at a supersonic speed. I have to attain way too much before I return, and I have no time to go slow!

"I will keep this in mind, Gus. I was still thinking about you. Like most of the other souls, you are very wise, but I never really understood that your elevated state makes you pass along your messages with a need for urgency. You have explained it rather well, and I will drop everything now just to interact with you."

That sounds good to me, Sunny.

"Is it you, Gus, who sends all the magical texts?"

Who else do you think is seeking attention?

"Thanks for confirming."

My mom and I have been master healers before, thus I need to remind her of all the power, potential, and knowledge she has within herself. Mom needs to devote way more time than she is currently to bring it all back to herself. She needs to back off gradually from her busy life, engagements, and interactions with most people. This needs to change, as more time must be devoted to this work, with only certain hours dedicated to the rest.

As I read Sunny's transcript of her session with Gus, I wrote:

I have witnessed this at the beach with Gus — how he interacted with a paralyzed dog who could still play, but Gus was very gentle with her. He also showed his compassion when he encountered a deceased dolphin and turtle on the beach.

In the session, Gus said:

Do *not* worry about yourself anymore, Mom. It will all be taken care of.

And I inserted the question:

How will this be taken care of? I do understand that experiences I have had have led me to move forward on my healing path at a whole new level.

In the session, Gus said to Sunny:

Mom needs to believe there are a few souls who are working toward making her better and assisting with her healing.

I wrote in reply:

Yes, I have had experiences with hands healing others. Your words took me back to how I was just a vessel and allowed what needed to come through.

Gus said:

I'm glad Mom is closer to her innate and inner self than ever before. She needs to have the same urgency I do.

I asked:

I am curious who is with you, Gus. Who is assisting you? I am a little uncomfortable with what I am about to say and not sure if this plays into my role as a healer: I was born on the same day as Thích Nhất Hạnh. Some time back, my husband and I went on a trip to Malaysia. While on the plane, I read a reading from a well-known medium who said that the word *mahatma* came up about me. I was stunned because of the coincidence of flying to Malaysia, where its Indian community calls wise ones by that name.

Speaking of my need to develop my skills, Gus said:

Only then can we fast-forward things and also my return. Mom needs to reach a certain level of competency, and it will not come along just like that. It is all around learning and awakening the consciousness that has been left dormant within herself. My mom needs the reassurance that she's on the right path.

I asked:

Gus, what do you mean by "right path"? With the Peruvian shamans? Are you encouraging me to move forward with them and incorporate my intuition and healing?

Gus said to Sunny:

Please ask Mom not to focus on herself as of today. She must go much deeper to explore the real her. I have been showing her visions from previous lives because some of them talk about and show the respect she had gained in the sect or the community where she was the master healer.

I asked:

Sorry, Gus, I do not recall what you have shown me from past lives. Can you be more specific? I recall I did a journey at a shaman workshop and wrote down some insights. At another time, I did an online workshop for two days on past lives. The teacher was Shama Viola from Damanhur, Italy. She channeled some past lives for me. [Here is when I began to realize that many of the unexplained images in Sunny's reported visions were events from my past lives — perhaps even from Gus's incarnations.]

Gus said:

Mom needs to forget who she is in this current life because she must do the awakening. We will connect at the firepit.

I asked:

Gus, which firepit are you talking about? The one being built at the beach house by the Zen room, or the one at the Atlanta house? Or are you talking about fireplaces? Or are you talking about the old metal firepit we would sit around? I don't think we have it anymore. [It occurred to me that any encounter with fire might invite Gus's presence.]

Gus didn't answer directly. He said:

Mom has enjoyed the status of reverence, but she has forgotten all of this in this lifetime. This is the only lifetime where a lot of time was wasted on being removed from her real identity. The birds I sent out for her are her protectors. They have also been brought down so that she may see flashes of her past lives. She knows more than she tells, for fear of being pompous or being misunderstood.

I reacted:

Yes, I felt this during my shamanic initiation. You are correct about me feeling pompous and misunderstood, for sure!

Gus said:

Mom, since when do you care about any of this? My message for you is strong: "*Now* and *now* is the time to act!" Devote everything you have toward this cause. The happiness and contentment this will provide will be worth so much more than your current efforts. Each soul must dig out the real self, especially when you have craved keeping the real magical powers of yours alive.

Sunny, Mom will completely understand what I'm talking about because she knows and feels it. She only plays her doubtful self, but she needs to believe in everything she thinks she is imagining.

I wrote:

Thank you, Gus! I do have to say it is something I have envisioned but have felt a bit lost on how to cultivate it to the highest healing powers in order to help others.

Gus said to Sunny:

My real reason for connecting — time and again — is to shake her up, to make her understand the real reasoning behind her being in this lifetime. Once she masters her hidden powers, her focus automatically will shift to bigger and deeper things. She has always been looked up to and still is.

Wake up, Mom! Wake up!

Sunny felt Gus's words were both spiritual and literal. At the time of this reading in Australia, it was 5:30 a.m. where I was in Atlanta.

Gus insisted:

Time is running out!

I wrote:

I am an early riser, Gus, as you knew when you were here. I need my rest to heal. When the time is right, I know I will be awakened at 5:30 a.m. If it is now, so be it.

Sunny said, "Gus showed me an image of a car skidding. I'm not sure if it has already happened or will happen."

Gus said:

Ask my mom about it.

I explained:

It has happened twice on separate occasions when a car has nearly hit me. And I do know sometimes I had to slam on the brakes when Gus was in the car! He felt the impact.

Gus said:

Calm yourself, Mom, and keep in mind the detachment. This is all a work in progress and needs a lot of determination and practice. You will get there, but shifting your primary purpose of being on Earth is more important.

You chose to be a mother, but your role is not restricted to just being a daughter, a sister, a lover, a mother, or a grandmother. Your role is denser and wider. Whatever you do in this life form will take you to a higher rung in the other realm. You decided to have all the relationships, but if you reflect on the depth of each, they were to make you learn the pain and grief of relationships that might have looked or sounded innocent. Even though you were living in the time, and with things that seemed frivolous, these experiences all play a role in shaping you in your dealings with others.

I wrote:

Yes, Gus, I totally understand this and why I chose my maternal family. I have so much to say about this!

Gus said:

Everything you were doing — and everything you will do — will be for others. There is never a *me* in it. There is always *them* in it. You will not be honing yourself for the *you*, but for *others*. That is primarily the role of everyone in this life.

We all know and understand that we get too involved in what we want to achieve, but the real happiness lies in understanding the others, in serving the others. The Supreme Power, the Universe, the Almighty, they're not there for themselves either. They are for the others.

All animals, they are not there for themselves, but are for the others.

I wrote:

Absolutely! It has always been this way, and I believe you understand what I am talking about.

Gus said:

You have to become the brighter light. You will shine beyond your inner circle, reaching out toward the farthest circle. You are blessed with a golden heart. You are doing a lot of thinking, doing a lot for others. You have to realize you are made for this work solely.

It amazes me that you have taken a little too much time to move forward. Do you understand now why I am desperate to give you the almighty push? Do you understand now why I need to talk to you more often? It is my role to awaken you and take you on this journey — the real crux of your life, the real reason to be "born," the real reason for devotion to your energy, your skill, and your power.

I wrote:

Yes, I understand what you are saying, Gus. I am a bit confused when you say I "have taken a little too much time to move forward." I am doing more work to understand and meditate since I have had my surgery. I'm beginning to understand that this surgery came at the right time, and I see how everything is unfolding.

I will need more guidance from you and Sunny. I do believe the universe will course correct me if I get sidetracked.

Gus asked:

Sunny, do you understand why I beg to connect?

Sunny said: "Gus, I do. I know it is something crucial, and this journey needs to be carried out with deep intensity and urgency."

Gus said:

My mom can't let the knowledge go unused in this lifetime. If unused now, its lack will affect her next and future lifetimes and their purposes. After coming this far and being a master healer, she can't just waste the learning and the teachings of her masters. Ask Mom to meditate deeply to understand what she was in her past lives. Those feelings will resurface. She will understand that every word I am telling you will be true. She will realize that, yes, knowledge is never wasted. The present learning is to revive the past knowledge.

You were talking to my mom about finding her niche and healing. Thank you for saying that because that's where she will understand her special touch — her niche. That's what she knows best and feels most comfortable with.

Mom, Sunny is here whenever you need her. Give up the social nuances and just reach out to Sunny, even if it is a daily need. You have no time to waste in being cultured or practicing etiquette about whether you will disturb anyone.

I want Sunny to hear how you are feeling. One session should only be about opening up to find your inner *you*. Nothing needs to be prepared. Everything, including some new realizations, will come out of you. They will be meaningful for you.

I agreed:

Okay!

Gus told me:

You are the energy that will *heal* others around you.

Mom, always believe that your Gus is with you. I think you can sense my urgency. You know this work needs a lot of energy. Keep at it because you will only be able to give what you have enough of.

Mom, tell me whatever you feel because even when you don't voice it, I know it. When you voice it, I'm able to bring out those feelings and emotions and realizations in you. You are beautiful. You trust every message I sent to you. Thank you for having the belief and faith in me. You know we are in this together. I have opened the gates to the real partnership between us.

I said:

I am willing to walk through the gates side by side with you, Gus.

Gus said:

We have progressed a lot since the first session. Then it was to establish who I really was and what I meant to you and others. Gradually you have understood that life is a progression. We must accomplish what we set out to do. Swiftness is the key. Unfolding of knowledge can take time and energy — and sometimes, a lot of it.

Thus, please give yourself plenty of appropriate nutrition. That is what will keep you going. Ask Sunny the real meaning of energy. Not having enough energy yourself can impair your work. Your well-being is directly proportional to the other person's energy and healing.

***Sunny suggested:* "Gus, let's do some visions."**

Do we really have to?

"Maybe the most significant ones from the past, the present, and maybe the future."

I can't disclose much about the future — only a little bit because I want my mom to ease up on her worries and thoughts.

Sunny, can we talk almost every day?

"Okay! I can try, but you need to be patient, Gus."

I don't have time, Sunny!

I injected this comment:

Gus is persistent, Sunny. I will let you decide how often you are willing to talk to him. I will let you know if he reaches out to me in an unusual way.

Sunny's Visions

> I see someone serving you something while you are seated in a chair. A dog leaps and is almost at your chest level. I see a female sitting on a chair, and the light shining on the person is either artificial or filtered sunlight.

JOY AROUND THE FIREPIT

Gus was always thrilled to ride in the boat.

I sense a significant memory involves speeding through the water on a boat. Gus is loving the wind on his face and feeling special. Gus asks another dog to play and to run together. An older couple sit at a table in a restaurant. You were not sure about the energy or spirits at your mother's house when you were growing up.

I note to you, readers:

Wow, so true! In my introduction, I only hinted at the trauma in the household during my childhood and teen years. I can't go into that here, but many of you will understand that having a close relationship — as I have with Gus — can soothe an earthly lifetime of pain.

As to Sunny's vision of the boat, we have an outboard at our beach house that tears through the water. Just as he loved riding in cars with the window down or in the golf cart, Gus not only loved the speed but also the salty seawater sprayed in his face.

Sunny continued:

> I see a female in a forest area stopping to feel the energy, a place with trees. I sense a magical feeling, almost like from the movie *Moonlight:*

Riding around in the golf cart was a guy thing. Jim drove, Gus navigated. I believe the golf cart is the "mechanical device" Sunny saw in her vision.

Spirits circle around you, almost like butterflies. Many of them, including a lady, step out of an outer layer, almost like stepping out of pants or high-top boots. I sense deep and restful breathing — a pet sleeping, maybe Gus. Someone is checking on or feeding a few animals. Gus is at the base of the stairs watching a lady descend from the upstairs floor of the house. I see a slow-motion jump onto a couch, long fur waving and the couch providing the soft landing.

I hear an interrupted conversation between a couple — the woman talking and the man listening intently. They talk around the firepit — a happy place. I hear that everything is for the children. They are hanging out with a bigger group of people in a tent, shaped like an inverted book.

I wrote:

All of these visions are very interesting — the boat especially, and the dog playing. The tent could have been my daughter's wedding at our beach house.

I was thinking about this a couple of days ago. Gatherings at the firepit were happy times.

Gus said:

Sunny, good health equals good reading, so take care.

Continuing Sunny's Visions

A woman lets go of things just because of family harmony. I heard, "Dad loves the outdoors. I would skip alongside him. He would even pick me up like a baby. He also expected me to train others like myself. Dad enjoyed as our relationship grew. I'm following Dad while he is sitting on something mechanical. Dad is practical and doesn't like dramas." You are going to meet a man who lived remotely, or in a village.

I note to you, readers:

This reference to "something mechanical" is our golf cart. As mentioned before, Gus loved riding in it, as he delighted being whisked along in any vehicle that went fast.

Sunny asked Gus, presumably about Jim and me: **"Have your parents known each other in past lives?"**

Gus answered:

Yes, they have.

Continuing Sunny's Visions

A man is swimming, involved in play fights. I hear, "Reconsider everything." I don't know if it's in a book or a movie. Dad pretends to be okay and fine, but he isn't. Gus is sending just too much information. I can't get it all because of the speed. It's now 4.30 p.m. your time today.

Gus told Sunny:

My mom is waiting for the reading. You'd better hurry up!

Sunny's visions continued:

I see loading something in the car, then a bumpy road. There is a forest area with tall pine trees.

I answered:

I found a beautiful place to walk in the backyard where there are lots of trees. Yesterday I felt compelled to walk through the woods and to the river where the sun was reflecting on my face and the water. It was so quiet! I meditated and felt peaceful. I've been seeing red-tailed hawks around our property for several weeks. They are flying low and showing up at significant times. Geese just flew over our house as well. Love the sound of their loud "barks" as they fly.

Continuing Sunny's Visions

> Gus is craning his neck to see the height of the trees. There is a serpentine wave touching the land. A couple hold hands while walking. Two birds of prey hover in the sky, but not too high. I see a box or crate. Gus emphasized its edges. Fragrance fills the air. Someone pushes a person in a wheelchair when it's dark outside. I hear, "Mom has to set up her healing station." Gus is cradled in someone's arm.

I wrote:

All of this feels good. Yes, my healing station is not finished at the beach house. The renovations have taken almost two years. We hope to move in there in late April. Gus, this was the house you were in as well, before the renovations. I see you there with us when you were in physical form and the memories we built together. I also see you there with Dad and me soon, you by my side while I do healing on people. This is what I have envisioned for two years now.

I can't thank you enough, Sunny. You are a blessing! You are also chosen for a reason.

Sunny asked, "Do you want to tell me the reason, Gus?"

He answered:

Time will reveal it to you. My mom thinks too much. She needs to be the doer. Get up! Face up, my beautiful girl! Look at yourself — look inside you! Hope is simmering and bubbling within you to achieve more. I will keep talking. This arrangement is perfect!

I wrote:

Gus, I want you sitting next to me while I do the healing work. Do you see what is being built?

From My Journal

February 6, 2024

I wrote:

Gus, today marks two months since your passing. I got up and meditated with the ñawis colors of the rainbow. [*Ñawi* means eye. In Andean philosophy, there are seven ñawis in our body, which are centers of vital, physical, and energetic functions.]

I kept telling myself I am a master healer. The energy was strong as I said this to myself. I was walking in the backyard and saw a tennis ball. I was pretending you were with me in body. When I got to the river and sat on the big log, I saw two more tennis balls! I had a big smile on my face. Stella is here today while Kim is at a conference in Ohio. It is bittersweet having your dog girlfriend here. I could tell she was somewhat confused as to where you were. In the car, she lay down in the back seat, leaning against the seat to pick up your energy.

FEBRUARY 6, 2024

Dearest Gus, I've been thinking a lot about you today. Actually, both Dad and I have had you in mind. It's just incredible how many ways you have shown me you're close to me. I trust your guidance, your love, and your compassion, especially when you talked about the firepit and about my understanding more of myself when in the presence of fire. I totally got it today. I listened to a podcast about the Year of the Dragon, which is this year. It talked about the fire and the dragon, about fire ceremonies, and about how seeing fire can really help you go deeper within yourself. It resonated with me so much, and I thought of you, Gus, when they talked about the ceremonies with fire.

I'm down here at the river behind our house at a spot I found where I could just sit on the log, thinking of you and crying.

I just had a session with Dr. Steven Farmer, and he did some healing for me. He has a dog named Scout who was in the room with him. Scout walked over and put his head on Steven's knee. As Steven was deep into the healing work, he said he saw you. I know I need to go through this process without you being here in physical form. I know this is all for a reason. I must learn to be more introspective. I get that. And I understand about the gates — all the challenging, and often fearsome, passageways — we must walk through together. I can't shake the feeling of how much I miss you, how I wish you were here with me. But I know you will be at some point in the near future. Thank God we have Sunny with us, and thank you, Gus, for reaching out to her and making me aware that you want to talk to her as well.

Don't ever stop. I always enjoy seeing those magical texts! I love you.

10

AHA MOMENTS

SESSION 7 – FEBRUARY 9, 2024

This session is another three-way conversation. Sunny sent me the transcript of her session with Gus, then I read through it and typed my reactions between their dialogue, as if I had been with them then. As you read how the conversation flowed, you would think we were all present at the same time.

Gus said:

Thank you, Sunny, for doing another session with me. You are a blessing not only for my family and me, but also for so many, many people and the lovely pets. You are the blessing and also the blessed one, and this work sends more blessings each and every day to you. Your karmic records are getting full of goodness. You have always been a giver, and it gives you more happiness than being a receiver. You should enjoy what you do, and do not let any doubt touch you. This is only the start. You will reach places or heights beyond your imagination. You do not know how everything has been planned with you and around you. Please do share this with my mom too. You are too shy and humble. You might be shy to speak about it.

***Sunny requested:* "Tell me one thing you like about me, Gus."**

There are a few, but I want to tell you that you feel for both the pet and the parent. You care about the thoughts, messages, and feelings. I know you think very highly of me, Sunny. This is exactly what I mean. You do not see me as in a dog's body alone, but as a soul that is enriched and enriches those who are around me. I have really started understanding your divine mystical ways of being and operation. I know I mean a lot to my mom, but I can see I mean a lot to you also. You including me in conversations from time to time is a great testament to your trust in me.

***Sunny said to Gus:* "Of course. I have seen the guru in you and love being the channel for your mom and family."**

I wrote:

I have such admiration and respect for the work you do, Sunny. I am glad Gus was able to confirm all of this with you. I feel your practice will grow and expand in ways you never imagined!

Gus said to Sunny:

I mostly talk to Mom because you can see she understands me on a deep and spiritual level. Can I please say to my mom that I'm very proud of her? Please tell her I am very pleased with everything because she has understood my attempt to shake her up and prompt her to awaken.

I wrote to Gus:

Yes, I have. Sometimes we all need a nudge.

Gus said:

I had to present myself in this manner because she's had to be reminded and pushed to become the *real* her. She is taking it all in, and nothing pleases me more.

Please tell Mom that whatever I have conveyed to her has both literal and spiritual meanings — and there are many connotations attached to the same sentence. There are so many aspects of any one thing because of all the experiences Mom has in her current life — and her other lives in the past. She will appreciate all those things that have dawned on her — and all those things that *will* dawn on her — as her *aha* moments! With health and its issues dealt with, she will rise like the phoenix. You will see her rise, Sunny!

I wrote:

You have provided most of the *aha* moments recently. I love how they have come up unexpectedly because this is the most authentic way of sensing a message. It is like I am doing something, and all of a sudden a message pops in my head to help me connect the dots. I now understand this, Gus.

Gus said:

Mom will also see herself rise. She has started taking things into her own hands. She has realized that tomorrow shouldn't determine today. Rather, today should determine tomorrow.

I wrote:

Yes, but by the same token, I do not want to force a task or thought until I feel it comes from the heart and not from my mind.

Gus said:

Tell Mom there is no linear path, and there is no one particular path. She is one of those blessed and chosen ones who will absorb everything from everywhere to make it her unique style. She doesn't need to learn: She knows it already.

I wrote:

Thank you, Gus, for saying this. I need to continue moving forward from my heart and intuition.

Gus said:

Mom will have some inconceivable success. She doesn't yet know that she has known this skill forever. The daughter she was talking about needs to be healed by her mom — I mean, *my mom*.

I wrote:

I will do this healing when the timing is right. I know my daughter will be open to receive from her soul and heart. As you know, Gus, it is the soul that teaches us once we awaken to the whispers.

Gus said:

I mentioned it the other day as well. Miracles will first be visible in all the people around Mom, the ones she knows. Then it will give her the confidence to soar like an eagle — majestic, powerful, unwavering, and undefeated. She will be the star who will be known for some of her magical work. This is not about developing a human ego because this work is only possible without developing arrogance or ego. It is the work that is carried out by the purest of pure souls.

I wrote:

Absolutely, but we do need an ego, not for greed but for purity. It is a part of us. I hope you understand where I am coming from. When doing something for another individual or individuals to help benefit their lifestyle or health, a kind deed is to follow through when it comes from the heart. Then let it go with no attachments.

Gus said:

Sunny, you haven't seen or met my mom, and she did not see you for a long time. You both felt the priority of intentions and thoughts. Mostly in life, we meet people devoid of societal values or outlook. You both connected on an energetic level. You could both sense truthfulness.

ced*I wrote:*

I feel we were destined to meet, Sunny. You could say we have a soul contract with each other, however it unfolds naturally.

Gus said:

My mom is a very guarded person. She may seem open, but she is very private.

I wrote:

Wow, Gus! So perceptive.

Gus said:

She shields her emotions and the family like a hawk. She's like a fortress that safeguards all those who reside within. Sunny, can you understand my description of my mom?

I wrote:

This is what we do when we love someone — just like I love you, Gus! In the physical form, both of us protected each other in complementary ways.

Gus said:

Mom can maintain going that way in terms of being protective. At the same time, she can release the tension around it because each person is being guarded by someone powerful. Mom, you do not have to carry that extra burden. It will dawn on you one day.

I smiled as I wrote:

Work in progress!

Gus said:

There are a lot of things that will start shifting when you trust yourself more. When you trust yourself, you trust others. Nothing is based on right or wrong, honesty or dishonesty. The people who dupe others have found an opportunity to learn a lesson, even if they feel victorious for some time afterward. One day, they will awaken. Mom, you directly or indirectly become the reason for their awakening.

I told Gus:

I appreciate your kind words.

Gus said:

With this knowledge, you may relax a little bit more. This is about being the one to generate an awareness for those who are lost in their lives.

I wrote:

I understand and know it is a gentle process for others to awaken. Some people are blocked in their awareness due to trauma, which leads to not trusting others, anxiety, depression, and, most importantly, lack of self-love.

Gus said:

For those who are nasty in their talk and actions, not one iota of effort needs to be wasted on them. It is their journey, and they will sort it out themselves. The nasty or selfish behavior is not projected at you, even if it feels that way. It is projected only at their own selves.

I wrote:

Yes, I do understand about projection, narcissism, and wanting power over the other, which is a form of projection.

When you withdraw yourself from the drama, you can watch it as the act of an external entity who is not connected to you in any way. That sense of indifference will actually make you understand, and that indifference will make you stand on your own, and stronger. This is where your growth lies: Your growth is in being able to see it all — the good, the bad, and the ugly. Yet the heart will always project only one reaction, and that will be of love. Just like Christ said, "Father, forgive them, for they do not know what they are doing."

I wrote:

Absolutely.

Gus said:

Mom, you will be much different because you don't have to forgive them. When you make the effort to forgive them, you are investing your energy in them, which will chew up your goodness.

I wrote:

I understand. There are situations when a person can be very abusive to another. I feel a person needs to work through the trauma in order to move forward. Or there are people who understand at a deep soul level why it happened. The abusive person may have had darkness and bad energy inside themselves because of how they grew up. Then it is time for the victim to move forward and make something positive out of this lesson to learn. Bring light to the dark. There is so much to say about this! It takes a strong and very self-aware person to stand up and break the karma in the family. Gus, I hope this makes sense, but I have a feeling you already know [my family history].

Gus said:

When you radiate and reflect only what you know best — which is love — your energy will be recharged, and you will rise higher into the purest form of being.

I wrote:

Exactly!

Gus said:

You are the symbol of *purity* and *strength*. Your powers would be so different. I wouldn't be surprised if you draw people like bees to honey. Because of your aura and your enlightenment, your community will be *born*. You have the time and the space for it to take place. Your actions will speak louder than words. You do not have to fake it to make it. Rather, become that person who has experienced tarnished relationships where every aspect and emotion were far from perfect.

I wrote:

Thank you, Gus! It is tapping into that sense of knowing and trusting it.

Gus said:

Honesty will bring more people to you. There will be many who want to move and change because of your attainment. There will be musical healings on the beach — communal healings — each one doing it to the other. You will be doing it for a few in an outdoor space near the fire, near the water, and near the forest. The healings will be in the open where the other person's soul can't escape the brightness and lightness of their being, thus becoming richer.

I wrote:

Yes, I feel the outdoor elements and nature will be very powerful for the client and for me as we connect to the spirit beings. I have been so blessed over many years with the animal spirit guides. It brings tears to my eyes when I give back and I honor what has been given to me. I call it reciprocity.

Gus said:

You are blessed, Mom, because you have a lot of support from many people who are with you always. Regarding learning about your soul companions, guides, or spirits, can you please do an activity with Sunny about this? She will help you identify them.

I wrote:

This brings so much joy to me. I can sense and feel it.

Gus said:

Once you know that, you will be able to take your guides to the healing sessions — the awakening sessions. You will teach and you will heal. You will do all that you want to do. I am there with you at every single step.

I wrote:

I love this, Gus, and I hope you are in physical form when you are ready to come back — all divine timing.

Gus said:

Reach out to those you trust — both living and in the soul. Develop your community. Be careful while choosing. You can only take those people who come devoid of any *drama*.

I wrote:

Oh, I hear you.

Gus said:

You cannot, at any time, waste your energy or effort on their tantrums. But as you progress, you will see a lot of them join with you. Practice each day, Mom. As you practice for your own internal growth, please practice outwardly too, in real time — on real people, plants, nature, and elements. You will be amazed. Whenever you let someone come on the journey, have those who will help you further your cause. As you do the healing work, let the air in, or do it outdoors where the energy is sent back to where it came from. A closed space can become very heavy, very soon, because of the residual energy.

I wrote:

I understand.

Gus said:

You can create that amazing flow of an energy circuit — an in-and-out path — so that weariness will have a negligible effect on you. You will excel in your creative ways of doing the work. If you do it with fire, you can direct the negative and dark energy into the fire to be consumed. If you do it with water or near water, you can let the bad stuff flow away. If you do it in the wind, it can blow the negative energy away. You will be shielded, and so will the others who are nearby or in the path of the negative energy.

I wrote:

Yes, I'm learning more. Knowledge is power.

Gus said:

I can't wait to do the energy dance with you, where we will be able to celebrate doing what we are doing.

I wrote:

Are you talking about when you come back, Gus?

Gus said:

This work doesn't have to be boring and on repeat mode. Instead, bring various techniques to the healing so that it becomes a permanent and holistic approach. The potential to make it interesting is immense. You will enjoy every single phase of it. This work will be the most noble and unique in its entirety.

You can't imagine how excited I am to be talking about the next steps already. Yes, it is all coming together. It will be *unique*.

I wrote:

Love!

Gus said:

We have the capacity to make it unique — a healing retreat. The whole Earth is your canvas. Welcome a selected few and give them nothing short of the best spiritual experience there is. I know you have similar thoughts, Sunny. It has to be holistic healing — healing of bodily issues but also of grief. There is a lot of pain, trauma, and abuse — and it can all be part of the healing. Healing doesn't necessarily have to do with ailments. But you can stop ailments and diseases from developing and spreading. Mom has already started working on the how and when.

It is so soothing to see the desire to progress. I want to send you a thousand licks, which are my kisses! You have got it all. You both are making me very happy and proud. I love you for *trusting* and *believing* in me.

Sunny's Visions

An object, which was to focus on, to pray with, or to be around it. There is a lot of glass in the building, and a young man is climbing the steps with agility. Someone is trying a yoga pose — an inverted body. Someone is sitting with her arms on her thighs, resting against the raised earth, which is part of a green oval with grass. Rebecca, I see you on a walk with dogs on a trail. A girl is calling out from behind for you to stop as she tries to catch up. I enter a space with a really low ceiling. It could even have been made out of a rock in a mountain. Two people are lying straight, not moving, wearing white clothes. Two massive dogs sit on either side — protectors of the entrance, as in Egyptian or Chinese cultures. Bullocks are ploughing. A highland girl is preparing and packing envelopes, then sealing them. Your brain is always thinking. I'm seeing the renovation work — someone getting onto one step, then hammering something, then moving onto the second step and repeating the same action. Gus is slightly ahead of his mom and turns to her as she watches the rainbow. I feel that Gus is also aware of the rainbow. A chimney is spewing smoke as from a wood-fired heater. There is a bench with one of its corners broken. Seems like curved concrete. Gus is involved in a game where he has to find something from three different spots or some objects. He is snuggled up to you as if he was feeling cold while sitting outside with you in the dark. I see a hammock or swing — someone is lying in it. There is a blob of water, on a table or on a gadget, where water shouldn't be. I see purple-colored dresses, and I hear bangles clinking in the background.

I wrote:

Gus, I need to read this several more times. Loving the piece about the rainbow. We are so connected to the rainbow energy.

Gus said:

I will connect again, Mom. I also want to release information a bit at a time after you have devoted time to understanding it. Please revisit the sessions after a few days. Again, it will generate newer perspectives. Stand proud and carry on. Great going! Very excited and happy, Mom. Take care! So much more to do.

I wrote:

I can't wait!

After I wrote my replies to this session, I wrote to Sunny:

Hi, Sunny. The day of the Lunar New Year brought in magical double numbers on my phone throughout the day! I saw hawks, which remind me of Gus. I would love to have a healing session with you. I will be curious what Gus has to say next and whether he is picking up what has occurred since the weekend.

From My Journal

FEBRUARY 10, 2024

I wrote:

Today was the lunar eclipse. Gus was on my mind, and the numbers 1010, 1111, and 1212 showed up on my phone yesterday. I kept telling myself I am a master healer. I went down to the river to walk after seeing an owl, which was an albino. I also saw a peregrine falcon, an eagle, and a vulture. It was so cool when I came to the river. There was a hawk standing on a limb with its wings spread wide open. I was thinking of Gus and had such a warm feeling within my heart seeing that. I'm going to write my comments on Sunny's notes of Session 7. I've already read it two or three times. I love how Gus shows up unexpectedly. Those are the best surprises.

FEBRUARY 11, 2024

Jim and I started looking online at Zsófi's website. We saw several puppies that remind us of Gus.

I decided to reach out to her because she has a litter coming in mid-March or April. I told her about Gus. I sent pictures of him and told her again what a wonderful dog he was. If she could pick out a puppy with his looks and mellow personality, it would be wonderful. By the time we get the puppy or dog, which would be in the summer, I feel it will be the right timing. But my heart still breaks for Gus today.

Today is a very tough day for some reason. I know one of the reasons he left was because I needed to move on without having him wrapped around my life. He wanted me to establish my own self with the healing process, and then he will be back. It's 4:10 p.m. I'm walking down at the river, and I was thinking about him and saying out loud, *I am a master healer!* All of a sudden, this hawk flew right in front of me like it was flying toward me. It was a confirmation that Gus was sending me a message. Every time he sends me a hawk, I think of him. He was standing guard yesterday as well. When Stella and I were coming out of the woods, I saw a huge red-tailed hawk sitting in the tree — the same tree where I often sense his presence.

In this same day, I was driving to the supermarket. I decided to switch the music to Pandora, which I never listen to while in the car. Nothing remarkable was playing when I got out to go into the store.

In the store, I saw a large woman with a newborn in her hands. Something nudged me to go over and ask her if she needed help. The infant was crying as the woman was trying to maneuver a large cart full of food and the baby stroller. Her hands were definitely full, and she seemed stressed. I rolled the cart to the women's bathroom for her so she could go in and breastfeed her baby, then said goodbye and took my groceries back to the car.

When I started the car, our song "Over the Rainbow" immediately started to play. I knew it was a sign from Gus.

It made me tear up because today was one of those grieving days.

FEBRUARY 14, 2024

Sunny did a healing on my body this morning. She said Gus was trying to interfere because he wanted her attention. Then I was texting with Kim's friend Ryan. He was asking me how I was doing. I put my phone down right after I told him I would contact Zsófi about getting another dog like Gus.

As I reached down to grab the phone again, I saw a new text message:

"I'm just"

I knew this was Gus's way of getting my attention. Obviously, he is not getting attention from Sunny.

But it's all good. Sunny had assured me she would reach out to him. I'm curious to know if he has a sense of what's going on. Today I saw the numbers 333 and 444, then 1010 this evening.

Today is Valentine's Day. Since the weekend, Jim and I have again been looking on Zsófi's site for another dog. We asked to see pictures — and wow, there are some who look just like Gus. I see him coming back when the litters are ready! I *miss him* so much, but feel better now seeing pictures of dogs who come close to his personality and looks. I read more about the life of these dogs at Zsófi's farm in Hungary — so similar to our activities at the beach house.

Sunny reached out yesterday about a body healing that I asked her to do. We both felt Gus was guiding us to do this. Today we were texting, and she said Gus was asking her to speak again. I am most curious if it is about searching for another dog. Sunny has no clue about that, and I am wondering whether he will talk about it.

It is mild weather here — an absolutely beautiful day. I took a nice hike for the miles at the river, to the same place where Gus and I would go. It was *so* nice and enjoyable! Tomorrow will be another follow-up with the doctor about my surgery. I hope I get a good report.

FEBRUARY 16, 2024

Early in the morning, I came outside to meditate. I looked through the trees toward the river and saw two red-tailed hawks and an eagle. It's the first time

I've seen an eagle from this viewpoint. It was a beautiful moment, and I started meditating on the rainbow.

Seeing an eagle isn't all that unusual at the beach, but they seem to come closer to me now that Gus has passed.

Good morning! The energy feels very, very good!

I'm at our house in Atlanta, but Lauren was at the beach house this morning with Jim. She dropped off her cat Myla before leaving for Europe on Monday. Jim took her through the house to show her the progress on the renovations. He wanted to show her the Zen room, and as they entered, Lauren looked out the window and an eagle flew over the marsh. We all feel that was a sign from Gus. The day is not over.

FEBRUARY 17, 2024

Jim is back now. We are both returning to the beach house tomorrow.

As I was sitting there, a text appeared on my phone:

"Pop"

It was one of those *aha* moments! Whenever Gus and I would sit by the firepit, a *pop* noise from the burning coals would come at the most significant comments during our conversation. It was so wonderful talking to him through the fire. He'd often spoken about how fire and firepits were so much fun for him. We shall see what will transpire as the day goes on. I will soon be walking on the beach and no doubt we'll see all his favorite doggy friends.

I also noticed a comment he made in Session 6. Gus, I'm going to make a note of that and make Sunny aware of it for when you communicate with her.

11

WHO COULD BE HAPPIER THAN ME?

SESSION 8 – FEBRUARY 19, 2024

This session is a conversation between Sunny and Gus. I add my journal entries at the end.

Gus said to Sunny:

I'm so much better after each communication session because my messages are reaching my mom, and who could be happier than me?

Sunny told him: "Yes, I can understand, Gus."

Gus replied:

Sunny, would you like to write that book in collaboration with my mom?

"Yes, it would be an incredible story that people would get to hear."

Oh! In that case, I can use many more ways to get in touch with both you and Mom. There are all the messages that my mom gets from me when I want her to get them.

"Did you mean the session when I was doing the chakra assessment with your mom?"

This is one of them, Sunny. As I have been saying for a while now, you have a significant role in our lives. Your role would be much beyond the animal communication work with me and being the medium between me and Mom.

Mom was blown away with the way her body spoke to you about its issues — and I know you were impressed with it as well. Mom is finally understanding that I will not stop until she takes the necessary actions. Please tell Mom that each sentence I have told her is a summary of an entire book. In other words, it's a compilation of numerous episodes and events. Mom, your well-being is paramount, but you must surrender to the All-Powerful to take you through this journey by dropping the associated fear. Your role for the greater good has not even started, and you needn't leave your physical body and go anywhere.

Put this worry or the underlying fear aside. Nothing is brewing or growing within your body. Please carry on with faith in yourself and those around you. You know I have been passing numerous signals to you using different souls and situations and synchronicity.

Yes, it is all a message from me for your safety, security, attainment, alignment, and reassurance. You have understood some parts of what I am communicating. As I have said before, please spend some hours each day to understand the other meanings behind what I have told you. Newer enlightenment will hit you like lightning. It will spark your brain. You know its significance. My message can revive you. You took it seriously and took your time to understand it.

A lot of your emphasis is on achieving your project, right? Everything you are thinking and what I'm communicating will make it come together. Your sudden awakenings are thoughts planted by me in you.

What is your worry regarding your children? Their life challenges are theirs alone. Sometimes removing your influence on them will not only offer you a different perspective but also a different outcome. Those friends who are a bit temperamental and unpredictable, they can be left to join you at a later stage. You haven't dumped them entirely, only left them for now so that they can do the catching up. When they achieve this, you can all vibrate at the same frequency.

None of the hurdles you're facing now are due to anything not going as per your plan. They're happening the way they should happen. Go with the flow. Do not resist anything. In life, especially on this path, logic has no role to play. Believe and trust your faculties. Go ahead with trusting the process laid out for you.

If you can't already see, then please let me reconfirm that everything has been laid out for you by us — by me and your other guides. Your brother and your father are there to help, but the major influence is your grandmother. Your mother is on other duties at the current time.

What are those new things you are drawn to? Understand that nothing — absolutely nothing — in your life is happening without our will and desire. Every single minute of your day is packed with things, including the revival routine.

I still find it difficult to believe your fear around a few things, especially when you understand that humans can't help in any way if it wasn't intended that way.

Sunny's Visions

> Massive, lightweight feathers — or clouds — come down to land on the water at your favorite part of the beach.

I note to you, readers:

I have a photo of the feather formation — taken before Sunny wrote this!

Gus said:

Sunny will finish your healing soon, but what you are achieving through self-healing is massive. You told Sunny about tenderness in your stomach. Tomorrow you should tell your brain to tell your body to start behaving and to settle the bloating and tenderness at the same time. There are certain herbs that can assist with this too. But your primary focus should be to command your body to heal itself.

In Sunny's vision she saw clouds descending on the beach. When it happened I saw Bobblehead!

Sunny will assist when I think you need further help. During the first session, I didn't want the full healing to take place. Thus, I guided the alignment, locating the problem areas and sources. If I had gone all the way, it would have taken away your confidence to self-heal. Do you want your brain to interfere, or would you like yourself to be the magnet to heal and self-heal?

If you have any burning questions, you can always ask Sunny. I know you have thousands of them! Many answers will unfold with time, but a few could be tackled now if you feel it is appropriate. You have been provided the tools and techniques, but the implementation has to be from your side.

Reach out and ask! Why would you hesitate to ask? Even though you know a lot, confirmation can make you relax and believe in yourself. As you take the steps to go down, you will be provided the path to come up, toward your progress and awakening.

By devoting more to yourself and to others outside of the family, you are not depriving the family of anything. Your family admires your resilience, your courage, and your love — and now they are almost there to experience all of this.

You had to undergo more emotional challenges than most others because you're learning how to help yourself to help those who are struggling in the very same areas or situations. You will be well equipped to provide that support. How can one provide genuine empathy when they have been spared the pain related to the same issues?

It hurts to see your inhibitions. You are great as yourself. You are already ready. You need to turn off a few taps and turn the others on for a proper flow of knowledge.

Why are you seeing more birds? Why are you seeing more of all kinds of species, both deceased and alive? Why do you feel your consciousness is getting sparked? Why do you think you are being told and shown a lot of things? What do you think? Why do you think you are being exposed to so much more than ever before?

You are more alert. You have to believe that life and nature offer your answers. You had once asked Sunny why I barked so much when we were on the beach. That bark was not a bark of frustration or of protection or guard. I was barking to tell you, *Look, Mom, isn't it all beautiful? Don't we all feel more alive absorbing the negative ions? The energy, the freshness, the imagination, the ideas, the being in the moment — excitement.* It was like telling you a story about how significant this part of the world or the city or the beach would be in our lives. It was weaving a fabric of excitement, enthusiasm, and everything in between.

I remember the laughter in your eyes. I remember the joy in your heart. I remember everything it meant. I will cherish it always.

There has been no day or time when I have really left your side ever since I dropped my body. As a soul, I can be in numerous dimensions at the very same time. What Sunny picked up from you was another fragment of you — as I am a part of you. It was the other you — your higher, elevated self, who knows you more than you know yourself. The elevated you wanted you to quicken your pace and deepen your belief — just as I told you as well.

You have experienced your elevated self already. It is pretty much to be understood that your less-evolved self will one day catch up with your elevated soul, which will continue to learn and grow. Thus, the dimensional difference will always remain, but it will also provide you direction.

Can you please acknowledge the higher-evolved self? Can you please ask for guidance when stuck? Can you please maintain this link?

It is important to this conscious connection because, when I return in a body, I will not be in a position to offer such rich and out-of-dimensional experiences, guidance, and support at the higher levels. You will then have to discover it for yourself. Your elevated inner self will guide, help, and support you. When counselors say, "Go inward to get your answers," this is what they mean. Ask your inner, your *you-yourself* guide, who knows it all and shows it all.

Some people do not have the time or experience to acknowledge it. The answers to the things you question, saying, "Oh, how do I know this?" are all provided to you by you, yourself, Mom. You are an extra-aware and awakened soul.

Just become the monk who trusts that their family is in good hands. Leave everything behind for attainment of the soul and the souls of the other beings. Please step back and look.

You have made your loved ones more reliant on you than anyone else. If you made them self-reliant, they would cope very well. In fact, they will also have their personal growth. Sometimes these things can't be done forcefully. Each soul will experience it at its own time — and sometimes not in this lifetime but in another or maybe in another one still.

Some in the family act like the anchors, and others are the drifters moving toward different locations, and none of it is right or wrong. If you are noticing more wildlife, it is me coming to you, showing you the support and love that you have with you.

Mom — my lovely mom — jog along the ideas.

Reach and grasp that which seems to be beyond control.

Continuing Sunny's Visions

> Someone is jumping through different levels, from the top to the bottom. What are those smells, Gus, that you get a whiff of? I see a candlelit romantic setting. Rebecca, you are barefoot on a damp surface, grounding yourself by connecting to the Earth mother. You are holding someone's hand as you both move through a crowded, tight place, making way for yourselves. You were overwhelmed then but had faith, just as you are in the same situation now. What is so precious in your bag, Rebecca, that your hand is resting on it for protection as you descend the steps? You are coming down from a spiritual place. Gus, ask Mom, what does she keep in that zipper bag? Break the protection chain that everyone is tied to. You are touching the back of a person. When they are lying on their side, your work (or a continuation of it) has begun.

I note to you, readers:

I'm stunned by the detail in Sunny's vision. The bag is where I keep my shamanic tools and textiles. The zipper bag is clear plastic, and I have my healing stones in there. Eventually I will place them on the altar of the Zen healing room, which is being built in the renovation project at our beach house.

***Sunny said:* "Thanks, Gus. Wow! You talked about really cool stuff today."**

Gus replied:

I always talk about great things!

"I will let your mom know tomorrow or the day after."

Mom is trying to be very patient, Sunny.

From My Journal

Febuary 21, 2024

I wrote:

I just had an *aha* moment. The synchronicity showed up again. Just loving it. Thank you, Gus. When are you coming back?

Gus, look at this morning! I'm feeling pretty good. I walked over to the house to watch the sunrise. Then I came back and started commenting on Session 8 that Sunny did with you. I still need to be convinced it's all you and not her interpretation.

I looked at my phone and saw 1010 and started laughing. Then as I walked all the way down to the end of the beach this morning and looked at my phone, I saw it was eleven o'clock. I thought it would be cool if I picked up my phone and unexpectedly saw 1111. I said I would love to see a sign from you. I'm always loving and asking and knowing it's you near me. As I walked all the way down to the other end of the beach, on my right was the place where you cut your foot. I looked at my phone just then, and 1111 showed up!

I love it. Gus, I love you, always communicating. More to come!

FEBRUARY 28, 2024

Right after I woke up this morning, I went over to the house to watch the sunrise and was talking to Gus. I walked the length of the beach, down to the beach club where Gus and I usually turned around. Just as I turned, I walked a few more steps and saw a red rose. I had a huge *aha* moment because it was close to where Gus smelled that first rose on the beach when we were together.

It was my birthday, and Gus was delighted to sniff this rose we found stuck in the sand on the beach.

As I was heading back from the store today, I heard our song, "Over The Rainbow." He is really reaching out to me today, and I love it so much.

I decided I want to title the book *Roses to Rainbow* I remember I saw two roses close to where Gus smelled the rose sticking out of the ground on my birthday last year, when he was still with me in body, on October 11.

Gus, this morning I was also thinking about your Labradoodle friend who lives in the condo we would pass by on our walk. I haven't seen them in a long time, but when I walked back by that condo today, that dog was standing in the yard and barking as if calling to me.

I am so in awe of all of the beautiful gifts you've given me this morning, Gus. I feel close to you again. I love you. We'll see what else transpires today.

MARCH 8, 2024

Dad and I were in the kitchen talking while he was cooking. We both agreed that we're going to wait a little bit longer, then we're going to ask Sunny if you are okay with us getting another dog. If you're not, Dad and I agreed that the timing is not right, and that is what you're telling us. I did tell Dad that

I definitely feel like your energy will be in the next dog.

Gus, we love you so much. It's just unbelievable that you are gone. Both Dad and I were laughing about the times we would bring back our groceries and how much you loved sticking your nose in the bags to smell them. Dad also talked about how you'd be there with him whenever he'd go out to fill the birdfeeders, following him everywhere.

MARCH 9, 2024

Gus, I asked Dad if he wanted to be more aware that you were around him. He said, "Nope, I'm fine just where I am." I asked him why he wasn't curious, why he didn't want you giving him more signs. He just repeated, "No, I'm fine just where I am." So I left it as is. I know you are with him. Perhaps if you were to give him signs, he would fall apart. I think he is being guarded, protecting his emotions.

Tonight I started working on Dad with the healing rainbow tools. I definitely need to practice.

MARCH 10, 2024

Today is a new moon, a very auspicious day. Kim's dogs Athena, Stella, and Tucker are coming over to play most of the afternoon because she has a photo shoot. Gus, I know your energy is going to be with them. More to come as the day goes on.

Gus, for some reason, you were so much on my mind. It was one of those sad days when I felt the energy was low.

Dad and I were sitting on the lounge together tonight looking at the stars and talking about you. We were again looking at Zsófi's website, seeing the dogs who look so much like you. Dad said, "I really missed the boy today." I told him I felt the same thing and wasn't sure why I felt so low, but it was nice to hear him express it with obvious emotion. He's normally pretty quiet about how he feels.

12
EXISTING IN THE EVERLASTING FLOW

SESSION 9 – MARCH 14, 2024

As Sunny reported to me in an email, this session began...

Gus said:

You took rather long to speak to me this time, Sunny!

Sunny responded: **"I let you take your time because most of the things have started aligning."**

I'm so glad my mom respects and listens to me rather intently. Mom's passion for and obsession with me, and everything related to me, is supreme. I love showing Mom and others in the house that I am so deeply connected to them. Mom has started on the journey with a lot of vigor and self-belief.

My mom and I have a lot of things in common. Apart from our looks, it is also a desire or a stubbornness. Once we put something in our minds, we execute it or try to execute what we believe in. Both of us can be opinionated, but we flow in joy and love for those who matter. We also give the benefit of the doubt to those who matter — and yet do not matter.

Our lives together have a deep purpose, and the connection will happen again soon — not straightaway, but soon. I have paved the way for her return — to her calling, to what she came to this realm for, to her true and innate self.

Mom darling is a darling for so many other people in her life. She was matured, just like wine or malt, for the best results. She was always spiritual and knew there was more to life.

But now it is on another level. I know she desires to meet me again — and to do all I have asked of her. But she must do only what she believes in. Every other detail she passes off, saying I will understand. That is my mom: She does what I tell her to, and believe me, her gut feeling or intuition is generally correct. My mom is skeptical, too, but there is nothing wrong with this. I also felt that way about some beings I encountered, but mostly I just went with the flow, or I created the flow.

You will understand what I mean by this, Mom. I will give both you and Sunny the sign when I'm about to return. I may need slightly longer than you anticipated, only because, as I have said in every single session, I will get you started off before I return, then it will be a collective effort.

My practice in this realm will enrich your experience of the same. I can't wait to return, either, but not as desperately as you want me to because I'm always with you. I will be taking a life form only for you and because of you. I know my signs astound everyone, and I just keep finding newer ways to make you all aware that there is no death: It is a continuation. It is a continuation of a growth and development, more experiences and learnings and the ultimate growth, which is closest to the Supreme.

I'm not there yet but have enough to be able to help you achieve your Akashic tasks and your karmic good. Most people do not really work on the next phase of life, which is in the other realm, and the one after, because they're not so foresighted. They only worry about the past and are involved in the immediate future.

The journey is unending. We would appear alive, and to the others, we would be dead. You had never imagined this phase to arrive this soon. Your hard work and heart's desire to achieve greater depths have driven you this far. Your unnecessary (but also, *not* so unnecessary) scare of health should not bother you. You know you are beyond that, and there is power in the energy within and around you.

For once, surrender to the higher energy, and just be guided because your future is destined. Only embrace it with utmost faith. You know that nothing can be altered if it is meant to go a certain way, yet a lot of energy is destroyed in worrying and thinking about it. Feel the removal of the extra burden by giving up yourself to the Creator, for there is no destroyer, as a soul can never be destroyed.

Believing it will make you and take you at an elevated level of being a healer. A healer's energy cannot be trapped in a body where fear exists. Fear drowns the energy, thus the work becomes harder. You would argue that you are human, and this is but normal. Mom, please understand that your energy is much beyond a normal human's energy because you are enlightened.

Living in fear is not desirable because the energy disappears from being very high to low. Do you think you have reached this far due to your brain-work? Absolutely incorrect! You have reached here because sometimes you were guided and directed; other times, you created the energy within yourself so you could rise up to the occasion. This is not being said in criticism, but utmost appreciation that you are closer than ever before.

You have the capacity to regulate the fear. Your numerous encounters with death were actually to make you fearless and not fearful. There is only one death of the physical body, and your time isn't here yet because it is not in your Akashic records yet. You have not even started what you have set out to achieve — the re-emergence of the healer in you.

You need to grow in the belief that your Gus knows what he's talking about. Normally, this information cannot be imparted, but I see at times how it has gripped you, crippled you from taking the deep breath of pure belief and trust.

This wisdom is beyond the physical world. It is beyond anything comprehensible. You need to soar like the eagle, the hawk, and the birds that you see high up in the sky. You must trust yourself and live without any fear. Let no fear grip you and tie you down.

I note to you, readers:

When Gus says he sees me "high up in the sky," I'm reminded of the vision I had during my initiation as a shaman practitioner: I saw myself riding an eagle in the sky and laughing with joy.

Gus continued:

What is nestled in you is nestled in everyone. Remember that you have come this far because of all the achievements in this life and past lives.

Can you please trust me? You believe that others in the family exist because of you. Rather, they exist because of themselves. Give them the opportunity to govern their destinies. Certain things and events make you feel you are or need to be in control of things. Please believe this: Nothing is in your control, even if it appears to be.

Let me disclose the real meaning of me leaving my body:

First, I had to assist, support, push, and help you from this realm.

Second, I had to show you there is life beyond the planet Earth in the souls' world.

Third, however hard you may try, you cannot stop anyone from leaving if it is their time.

Fourth, I've been trying to show you my magical and supernatural things to tell you and to make you feel that nothing stops beyond the barrier of the body. Everything is possible.

My departure had many lessons for you. I know you know it, but just think about it and let your fear disappear. Prior to our arrival in this life, we have all decided the day of our departure as well as our experiences. We understand the overload — or just the load.

I am very excited about your enthusiasm related to things that involved both of us. My favorite place is to be with you. My understanding of you is much deeper than your understanding of your own self. This was also the case when I was in a body form. This big shift will empower you extremely, and I know I am pushing you for it. But you will eventually have to do it yourself — to unleash the person you want everyone to know and to present to the world as a healer. A healer is nothing without the guiding light. The guiding light and energy show you the direction — at times, perhaps only as much of the direction as you can handle.

I know my obstinate self has put you in a rigmarole, much heavier or stronger than you have put yourself through or are ready to receive. We are not able to match our expectations yet.

I'm laughing about it because I'm coming across as a bully, and you need to go at your own pace. There is no need to slow it down, especially when you can decide to pick up your pace. But you will only do what you are comfortable doing.

This conversation may actually stop you to reflect more on it. Do you sometimes feel like me? Yes, but then you quickly revert to the present, when you are in your thoughts. Think about it. Think about being able to connect, heal, and expedite things, events, situations, and circumstances for all those who are living, as well as for all those who have left this realm for now.

You will find the awakening in spurts, just as you will accept one thing and then the next. Yes, I like the space you are creating for the both of us. I know sometimes you want me to be crystal clear in my messages. I'm trying to tell you things without breaking the protocols of this realm. Your interpretation is up to you.

I know I'm fixated on a few things. Please ask Sunny about my energy levels when I'm trying to bring about a major shift in you. You will be able to generate miracles in your own family before they become visible to others. You are very well aware that you are the vessel for the healing, and you said the same to Sunny. As long as you are the vessel, you will be guarded from anything attaching to your energy. You will be directed and helped.

The day you think you are the healer, the onus will be on you to protect your energy, your position, and yourself along with the karmic records and so much more.

Sunny is being directed by me for further growth as well. Her understanding of a few things will help you in your understanding. Whenever I said you both are connected for a reason, the reasoning and association are much deeper than you expected. You both need to truly and fully understand each other. You do not know each other well now, and the shallow understanding isn't helping in the process.

Each of you is totally different, and your outlook toward living and death (or transitioning) is very different. Surrender and see where it takes you both. I showed my patience only because of my personal agendas for Sunny.

This is just the beginning for you, Sunny, even though you want to help the animals alone. Every aspect of new siddhi [knowledge] will help you both as well. My excitement about everything associated with people on this journey is incredible.

You will have put a few thoughts together based on what you were told by your masters. You are able to understand the significance in your life. Put the knowledge not in a linear manner, but in a circular path, and it will make more sense to you. You will understand all that is currently happening.

Just carry on, Mom!

From My Journal

April 4, 2024

I wrote:

We are definitely in the eclipse season. The total solar eclipse will be April 8, 2024. It's been incredible, what has transpired this whole week. So many magical messages from Gus. You just cannot make this stuff up!

This morning I woke up and decided to walk down and put some birdseed down by the birdfeeders. I laid the seed container by the firepit, and on top of the firepit was a small stone shaped like a heart. I was stunned and started tearing up. I was so grateful for this message from Gus — from the universe. It was remarkable and astounding to witness this gift for me.

I remember how Gus would jump up on the firepit along with Stella to look for chipmunks, and that's why this discovery reminded me of him. It was just like he was saying, *Sorry! Digging in, looking for the chipmunks, but here you go, Mom. Here's your heart.*

I believe the meaning of this symbol also relates to when Jim and I were in Peru in 2017. I found a small heart-shaped stone on our anniversary. I had saved it over the years, and I used it as one of my healing stones, but two weeks ago, I was out in the back meditating, and I noticed there were cracks in the heart stone. Here was a powerful symbol of the heartbreak I've had since Gus has been gone. It was a deep-seated depression. The grieving process has been hard. But today here was a heart stone just about the same size, and I immediately thought, *My heart is whole now!* Gus is saying he loves me and my heart is healed. This was such a very profound, stunning, and remarkable message.

I took a picture of the stone, then I asked Jim to come down and look at what I found. He was stunned. He said, "Wow, that's weird!" He insisted he'd never seen that stone on top of the rock. I hadn't either. It was the only stone that didn't look like the firepit rocks.

I discovered this heart stone atop the firepit at our house, a place where Gus and I often sat together, watching the dancing flames.

13
THE WEB OF LIFE

April 7, 2024

Sunny emailed me:

Hi, Rebecca. This message from Gus (find it below — Session 10, dated March 9, 2024) was delivered nearly a month ago, but somehow I had no energy to send it, which is rather unusual. Today, I had not even thought about sending it, but somehow I was guided to do so.

I was the calmest and absolutely at ease as I wrote it out. I knew that the day was today. In general, more than the sender, I believe such messages must be timed well for the receiver. I was thinking deeply about it, and I realized the visuals might not have made sense to you earlier. But now I think you can validate the parts.

Also, there is a strict protocol in the other realm about telling the future.

This session has sent my mind reeling! It is my absolute favorite. It is so deep, and I can't forget the laying out of this cosmic relationship and connection. Previously, I had this really strong intuition that Gus would either stop at the tenth or eleventh session. He hasn't been asking me desperately anymore.

I have said a few times that he wants me to finish and start practicing what I am seeking certification in. I know we will have a humongous revelation, and I also believe it will help a few others with the healing they need. This patience is for his mom too.

SESSION 10 – MARCH 9, 2024 (SHARED WITH REBECCA ON APRIL 7, 2024)

Gus said:

Thank you, Sunny, for waiting for another time to communicate. I enjoy that you are playing such a crucial part in this journey of my mom. She is a fine woman, and whenever you both meet, you will understand the importance both of you will have in each other's life.

Your association has already begun, but meeting in person would have an astounding impact. Isn't it beautiful and mystical, how energy connects — especially of those on the same journey and those who meet while in the lifetime of gaining experience? You would see it unfold in a rather dramatic manner.

As I have always said, this is only the beginning. We really appreciate you stepping in and becoming a part of this beautiful journey. The path that both of you are on does not have an end date of learning. It is learning in progress with faith in your hearts.

It is not about waiting for the big day because you would have to create a big day yourself: Belief in thyself, trust in thy Superior, magic in thy soul — results in all those you touch at an energetic level. The path is paved, the wait is here, the action needs to be implemented.

Mom has set her timelines for things, which is great because they have become her goals. In the interim, it is very significant because it is the preparation ground. It is the trial ground. It is the space that connects the dormant to the eruptive. It all takes time to progress, to unfold, to materialize, to action, to result.

No time is a long time, and no period is a no-action period. The physical self can't and shouldn't be a hurdle because facing things is rather important.

A lot of things that I know don't need any special attention. The physical self has been cared for. That, as I always say, I am there to look after. I'm also going to look after the other things, but I want you to take the lead and initiate it.

Everything in life is around timing. My birth and my departure were both timed, keeping in mind all the other things that were associated with it. Mom, my purpose with you is still unfinished. My return is inevitable, but it will depend on your timing. Honestly, that time is set, too, and this push is also a part of it for the timeline to be followed. Do follow your heart, and it is rather wise, but sometimes remove yourself from the body and reflect on your role and contribution. I am going to be with you each step of the way.

I have shown your past to instill faith in you. The past can't be forgotten. You will be more capable than anyone else because learning can take years and lifetimes. Your skills only need a light brushing up.

Sunny has said the same to you before, and she is waiting for the floodgates to open for herself as well. The more she involves herself in worldly tasks, the longer it will take her. She's aware, yet it is taking longer than needed.

Mom, our spending time together, our journeys, were the trust building and bonding activities. Had they not taken place, you wouldn't have approached Sunny. Finding Sunny was all part of the plan. Soul finds the medium, and not the other way around.

For Sunny to be a medium, a lot of changes had to take place in her own life. Sunny had to beat her grief to be able to reach here. I'm telling this so that you understand there is a web, a broader context. Everyone from different tangents is brought into the web to help weave the circumstances, thus the situation or role.

Even those who were not great contributors in the fabric of life have to be appreciated. Each one of them allowed you to grow, to understand, to face this web called life and its lessons. No one does anything in isolation, even if you think at that time you were doing so. When that isolated move becomes a collective effort, it brings about a profound change. All those who will be healed through you at this stage have no idea what awaits them. This is the primary reason to trust every emotion that arises within you and in others — the good, the bad, the ugly, the beautiful.

The beings on this planet are all interconnected through this web, which includes all the species, and no species stays the same or stagnates, for there is no stagnation. Even slow action — and no action — is also an action.

If you look at the spread-out web or fabric with all the connection points, it's mesmerizing. These connection points emerge in different dimensions. Connections include the ones who have transitioned, those who are about to transition, and those you have not met in this lifetime because they transitioned before your arrival, such as your ancestors. Do they have roles in the current connection points? Yes, they play highly significant roles in your current life.

Your consciousness is not yours alone but a collective consciousness. The collective makes you the real *you*.

Why am I talking about this? It is to make you understand and thank all those who have added to your *today*. Species other than yours are also a part of all these experiences. The birds who greet you, the four-legged creatures who meet you — the love in their eyes isn't because they are these amazing creatures. But connections have many more aspects apart from love, including experience, emotions, and the living of those emotions, as well as, of course, the feeling of love that is reciprocated — be it to guard, to greet, to respect, to help, to make more connection points.

The most powerful emotions are rather important — including those of loss, fear, hopelessness, and anything that will make you fall. The resilience, living through the world's scenarios, the fear, the sickness — all these experiences occur to extract the "gold" in a person because that part of the web or fabric needs to get richer.

You have to be significant in someone else's life, even if it is to say one word or a sentence when you come together. This realization will always make you appreciate *everything* — every human, every element, every atom, and every particle.

Now you can understand all the past sessions at a deeper level. The learning runs even deeper at an atomic level. The "energy" we sometimes talk about in a matter-of-fact, offhand manner involves much more than our simply breathing and our bodies performing. The *cosmos* is one *big* family. We are all related to each other at multiple levels.

I know what I am unfolding is rather complex, but if you understand this, you will be more open and receptive to everything within yourself and outside yourself. You will appreciate all the other layers around you, which helped make you who you have become.

In your past lives, you have seen simpler associations because of less complex relationships or more awareness. The collective is more powerful than the individual. In the past, we heard things like, "It takes a village to raise a child." It literally was that way. Now we have started becoming guarded, pretending to be nonintrusive in the name of privacy, for example.

My role in the family's life, and even after the departure in the lives of the other souls, is huge. Our energies are magical strands of knowledge and information because we rest in a high energy and collective energy realm. You could look at this realm as an enclosed pod, an area with high, super-high, and elevated energy. Learning and support continue from this realm, not only for our immediate loved ones, but also for anyone we meet at the connection points in the web of our lives.

I'm helping a few people from here. I'm also elevating my own knowledge, helping souls and energies in this realm, and the cycle continues.

Staying happy and contented amplifies the energy in a body, even if the person's lifestyle has minimal resources. The whole picture has been displayed in front of you. Gauge the ways you feel best, and use those methods to elevate your happiness and purpose. For example, *gratitude* is huge in shifting the energy orbits. Being grateful for every learning experience and exposure will set you apart from others. Believing in this advice is very important. You may have known or heard about something similar before, but I'm talking about living it and carrying it to the next lifetime.

Sunny's Visions

> Rebecca is performing a healing. Your hand is moving high and low toward the person's chest or stomach area. You are traveling in a boat, sitting and absorbed in your thoughts, wearing light-colored clothing. You are coaxing a cat to move, a deity with a flower at its feet, a lotus with huge petals. I see a waiting area. You are moving chairs. There is a bubble-like scanning machine. I see a radi-

ologist and a doctor talking to two people — you and someone else. You prepare a protection circle before you go there — right up to your stomach from the top — very similar to the machine bubble. Are you scared? Gus said it is unnecessary and turned his face. You are eating probiotics. I see young children, maybe eight or nine years old, a boy and girl sitting in low and sunken chairs. A gearstick is being moved, and a hand opens as if taking pressure off. Someone is checking the underside of a vehicle. I see a forest area, a cat sleeping in the sun or a warm place.

APRIL 7, 2024

I emailed Sunny:

Hello, Sunny. Thank you for sharing this beautiful and thought-provoking message from Gus. I have read it twice and will process it all. Later today I will come back to read it again, and would love to share my comments.

One question I do have now is: Why did you decide to send it now? Something very significant happened this morning while I was sitting outside absorbing the sunrise and watching nature wake up.

I witnessed a message I have never encountered, and I felt strongly it was from Gus. I am curious if it is tied into your decision.

Sending love your way.

Sunny replied:

Hi, Rebecca. Here is the surprise element. It wasn't meant to be delivered earlier, and you would best know the reason. I tried my hardest and set aside time to write it up, but it just wouldn't happen, and today it was meant to be. Some of the visions are no longer current, but it conveys what was going in Gus's mind at that stage, so in a way very relevant. This reading also marked the finishing of my diary, so it sits as a significant last entry. I don't know if there will be any more of these sessions, but time and nudging will tell. I hope you enjoy it. I quite enjoyed the explanation as I was writing it, and I think Gus explained it in much detail through the feelings and emotions.

Warm regards.

From My Journal

April 7, 2024

I wrote:

I sent Jim the response Sunny sent back to me. As he was reading it, our first hummingbird flew right beside him by the feeder. He also saw a red-tailed hawk on the limb of the tree out back. It landed on the ground inside the fence, and it spread its tail feathers out as it reached the ground.

I drove to the river this afternoon to walk, and I saw a possum stunned, suffering in the road. I pulled off to figure out a way to move the animal off the road. A couple pulled up to help me. They got it off the road, and we all knew it had gotten hit and was suffering. But we felt it could pass away in the elements it knew best — the woods.

After they left, I walked and came back to it. The possum was breathing heavily, and I teared up because it was still suffering. I put my hands close to it to help it go over to the other side. I said a prayer and left. I did not want to add stress to its passing.

Today has been filled with interesting events. I feel

Gus has been speaking to both Jim and me today — before the total eclipse tomorrow.

As I am writing this, I realize — with all the synchronistic events that have happened this morning and this afternoon — today is the four-month anniversary of Gus's passing.

When I woke up this morning, I felt really good. I woke up early, got my coffee, and happened to look at my phone, where I saw the Session 10 email from Sunny. My heart sank a little bit, but I decided to look at it after drinking my coffee and doing my ritual of going outside and watching everything wake up.

I was going to do a quick folding of clothes, but I chose instead to go outside. When I lay down on the lounge, all of a sudden, a blurred form flew out from the right side of the house, then a hawk, then another bird. Three birds landed on the same tree limb, and I realized the first one I saw — that blur — was a barred owl. It seemed so odd that they weren't being territorial with each other. My immediate reaction was that this was definitely a message from Gus. Then one hawk flew off the limb and the owl stayed. Then the other hawk flew off to another limb, and shortly thereafter, the first hawk joined it. I figured they were male and female (they mate for life). I hear the owls hooting at night.

I wasn't sure what this message meant. I reached out to Sunny and asked her why she felt she needed to send Session 10 now instead of earlier. I saw she had actually communicated with Gus on March 9, 2024.

As Jim was reading the message from Sunny I sent him, a hummingbird came up to the feeder. I'm thinking these are messages from Gus and trying not to overthink it, just allow it to be.

Does this mean Gus is not coming back? Does this mean we do not have an opening for the book? Throughout all the sessions, Gus has always talked about his return. Plus, Sunny and I were texting the other day about the book. She thought the opening would be the story of Gus's return.

I told her I wanted to tell her what Jim and I are doing about adopting another dog. I want to wait until everything unfolds with the right timing. So many things seemed to depend on Gus's return.

So far, I have not responded to Sunny about the messages in Session 10.

14
ENERGETIC REFLECTIONS

APRIL 14, 2024

I emailed Sunny:

I hope all is well at your end of the world! How are you doing? I wanted to share what is going on with me. Thank you for sending this [Session 10] from Gus. It is very deep and intertwined with love. I am sure I will continue to absorb at a deeper level the magnitude of this message. I say this because I finished listening to this extraordinary podcast with Robert Comber and astrologer Pam Gregory. On May 1, Robert is launching his book, *Lost Octave.* It is a phenomenal conversation about the new human, the Lemurians, different healing modalities, and so much more. If you have time, I would highly recommend listening to their podcast.

From My Journal

April 14, 2024

I wrote:

I had another initiation Yachay [means *to learn*] Karpay yesterday, toward my certification as a paqo [shaman] practitioner. Yachay Karpay is knowledge and intuition that is the intelligence of the ancestors and Universe to fill the body with sacred light. The practice was done remotely. The paqo starts with a beautiful ceremony asking Pachamama to bring Apus Qoyllur sacred mountain to unlock my belly button by the spirits of Hanan Pacha. This work will reconnect me with Pachamama, the land where I was born. The lock of my belly button will be opened by the spirits to create a channel between my Pachamama and me.

Then the transference of wisdom will start.

Pachamama has energy lines much like the seven chakras. This arrangement is related to the rainbow energy. I am dressed in white for every initiation and I meditate lying down, in nature if possible. I begin by using the kintu in a prayer to ask for permission to receive wisdom and intuition. Then I put my mesa, a kind of pouch, on top of my belly. The mesa has my healing stones and tools in it.

For you, readers:

The kintu is a talisman that has a grouping of three coca or bay leaves with the stems pointing down and the leaves facing up. The three leaves represent the upper, middle, and lower worlds. The leaves also represent the physical, energetic, and spiritual body, as well as the body's three major centers — belly, heart, and mind. Kintu prayer rituals are done by kneeling or sitting on the ground with eyes closed. In using the kintu, a shaman is calling the spirits of the Apus sacred mountains of Pachamama and opening themselves to receiving deep connection.

The night before, I had asked Gus to be with me during my initiation. At the start of the initiation, I looked out, and immediately a red-tailed hawk flew across the sky, so close to me. I knew it was Gus's presence. I journeyed during the initiation, which lasted an hour. It was so profound and magical!

I immediately felt the initiation was over, and when I woke up, the red-tailed hawk flew across the sky again!

I knew it was another message from Gus.

I lay there for a bit, absorbing the compelling initiation. I felt led to put on some music, and the first song that played was, "Over The Rainbow." As I was about to type a note about how magical all these synchronized events were, the red-tailed hawk flew across the sky yet again — so close — and made some chirping noise!

Wow, just wow!

How Gus and the divine are showing up!

I feel immense gratitude and wonderment.

I am on my third module of the shaman classes, which will be complete the first of May. Then I will get my final initiation to be a certified shaman practitioner. I am gaining other knowledge from different masters as well to intertwine it all.

I am building a web of knowledge. The spider! Blessings!

April 20, 2024

Today and tomorrow are the first time Jupiter and Uranus will be in Taurus since 1941. Last night Kim was supposed to come over, but she wasn't feeling well and I was actually very relieved. I told her to stay home because I really wanted to sit outside, relax, and just be. I stayed outside till 9:30 last night watching the clouds moving over the almost full moon. It will be full on Tuesday the 23rd. It was such a beautiful sight. It was almost like the clouds were opening up a portal to the moon. I could see golden light around the clouds. I felt immense gratitude, and knew I am a healer. I just knew it. It was a feeling so deep within me, and I had tears running down my face.

All of last night felt as though I were going through other dimensions, understanding the stars and the golden light. I felt like they were right there with me, embracing my heart. I watched the wind blowing the tops of the trees. It was as though they were dancing back and forth.

April 21, 2024

I am blown away by what happened around 5:30 p.m. today. I came home, and our class was canceled. So, I was thinking, *Okay, when am I going to go down and walk by the river? Or go to the grocery store (which I really don't want to do)?* I was really missing Gus and was yelling out to him, *Oh, Gussy!* as I would do. I kept saying that, and I really felt him there. So I decided to go outside and feed the birds some worms. I had my back to the woods because I was looking up at the clouds and noticing how pretty they were. Then I heard this screeching noise above me, turned around, and there was a red-tailed hawk flying low in circles above me. I knew it was Gus because I was calling his name out and was missing him so much.

He heard me. Wow, I'm blown away. I love you, Gus, and miss you.

April 29, 2024

I was walking on the beach, thinking about everything that went on with Kim. She and I were walking with Bandit, her boyfriend Chris's dog, and Truman, Lauren's dog. Bandit bit Kim when she tried to break up a tussle with Truman. So much drama! We could have gone from a little bit of chaos to a lot of chaos, drawn a lot of attention to the situation. We didn't know whether Kim's friend Gabe was going to come back here with Truman to celebrate Kim's birthday and my Mother's Day. But we ended up fixing it. Kim's wound was not serious, but the celebrations did not take place — and I wasn't disappointed.

I was still thinking about it as I sang to myself, "Don't Worry Be Happy." Was thinking of Gus as I was walking on the beach. I decided to turn on Bob Marley, and the song "Three Little Birds" came on. Again, everything was going to be all right. This was right after seeing the crow this morning and yesterday. I'm seeing all the synchronicity of this. It made me laugh.

I just love it. Gus communicates through songs.

April 30, 2024

Yesterday I went over to our renovated beach house. Gus was strongly in my mind. As I was watching the sunrise, I heard a noise to my left, and there was a crow standing on the chimney right beside me, watching the sunrise as well. I was done with my meditation, but it brought me such joy to see this because several crows had stayed the entire time. Then the last crow took off and circled way above the ocean.

This morning, I was at the beach again to watch the sunrise, and I was on WhatsApp communicating with some of the people in my shaman workshop. The conversation was about a woman whose parents died by suicide, and she had an eating disorder. I immediately responded that it sounded like what I'd been through with my parents. I heard the noise again. There was the crow standing on the chimney as if it was trying to tell me something. It was cawing, but not loudly. I began to wonder whether the crow was becoming my spirit animal, and whether Gus was speaking through it.

MAY 2, 2024

I had a session with Steven Farmer, who is one of my mentors and a shaman practitioner. We discussed the book and my feelings about Sunny collaborating with me on it. I let him listen to a message she had sent. He said it was gibberish and that I needed to let her go. He felt like she was manipulative. I've been feeling that way for over a month, but I needed an outside opinion, guidance from another author.

I was feeling a lot of grief because I knew in my heart Sunny and I were enmeshed, and it was not healthy. Letting her go would be like I was grieving on another layer, like letting go of Gus. After all, she has been the vessel of communication with Gus and has given his messages to me.

Steven said Sunny's time with me has been served. It's been a grieving process for me, and I should start moving forward. I was so devastated on Thursday. I didn't know how to cope with my emotions and my feelings.

May 3, 2024

I woke up today, which is Kim's birthday, still feeling out of sorts and asking my spirit guides for clarity. I still feel very unsettled about it all. Then I chose to take a step back and not respond to Sunny for a while — not until I know I am confident in my decision one way or the other about working with her on the book. Steven did give me another author to consult with if I wanted to look her up.

I was feeling extreme sadness yesterday and strong emotion as I talked to Gus. As I drove, I was talking to him, and our favorite song came on, "Over the Rainbow." Later, a John Legend song came on that has roses on its album cover. It was so profound because I don't hear that song often, but it does come on at very magical and compelling times when I feel such a strong connection to Gus.

May 12, 2024

Today has been an interesting day with Gus communicating. Yesterday I was thinking I had not heard from him since his magical texting. On the family group text thread, Lauren was talking about Truman coming to stay in the hotel for the wedding of my nephew Alan Richmond and Lauren Moody. Then an emoji, a salamander, popped up as if it were my reply to her. But I never selected it. Then I responded to another group text and another emoji came up before I typed the sentence. Then in a different response, I asked Lauren if the salamander had shown up again. There was a laughing emoji when I was getting ready to look at her response, which was a smile. These emojis couldn't have come from me because I never touch that part of the keypad.

As I was walking in the neighborhood, I was thinking of Gus. I got to the spot where Jim would drop him off sometimes, and I just happened to look up and saw a hawk in the tree.

I'm loving the way he communicates. I love you, Gus.

MAY 19, 2024

This morning started out really good. I decided to start reading all of the transcripts from Sunny on my laptop. I wanted to see if there was a correlation between my shaman initiation and anything Gus had said. As I was reading from the laptop, I decided to go inside to get my phone because it was on the charger. I'd been reading Session 7, which was about Gus and the rainbow. When I reached for my phone, Facebook sent me images of rainbows from my memory album. Gus was in one of the memories — a picture I took — with a rainbow behind him. I teared up because I thought I knew he was right there with me.

Our cat Samantha sat by me, rubbing her body on my legs. Then I went back outside and decided to finish reading the transcript. Samantha followed me out and sat with me, rubbing up against me because she knew intuitively I was feeling sad. She was trying to comfort me. Then she decided she wanted to go back in, so I let her in.

About ten minutes later, Jim came out and said, "The chipmunk is out. Can you help me get it?" The backstory on this is a bit of light drama. Eight days ago, a chipmunk somehow got into our workout room. We knew it was there, but it was hidden so well we couldn't catch it. Today, Jim was in that room and Samantha was outside in the yard. Then he saw her scamper over. She sat down, looking at him from the other side of the sliding glass door. She's never done that before. She seemed to be staring intently at him. It's certainly common for a cat to want to be let out, but urging us to let her in? So Jim opened the door for her, and she ran straight to the chipmunk's hiding place. She came out with it dangling from her mouth. Jim rushed around to find a towel, the cat let go of the little creature, and he put a towel over it, thinking it was dead. But, moments later, the chipmunk slipped out of the towel and was running around the room frantically. That's when Jim came out and asked me to help him. The drama ended when Jim managed to set a live trap. We were able to chase the chipmunk into the trap and then released it in the backyard.

After we caught our breath, Jim and I had to laugh at this. He remarked that Samantha knew it was her job to rescue the animal. We agreed that she must have been channeling Gus, who guided her to do it.

May 20, 2024

I reread Sunny's conversation with Gus in Session 9.

Then I emailed her:

I wanted to take my time with reading this session, after things have settled down. Friday I had a huge initiation to be a ñusta paqo shaman, which means being able to do healing work with the rainbow colors and chakras. It was time spent alone and in nature for several days.

Now I am with my daughter and her dogs at her mountain house, which is wonderful. I needed to get away to another place in nature where the energy is totally different. Gus used to stay with me here when he was alive. Now I have felt him here again, and he has given me messages along the way.

I was chuckling at some of the comments I've made about his messages through you, Sunny. My curiosity and desire to understand how you actually receive these messages from Gus is really piqued. Does he speak to you directly, or do you interpret in your own words what you feel you are hearing and seeing — or however you channel the messages?

Sunny did not answer me right away, and I must say I was disappointed.

May 28, 2024

Yesterday was Memorial Day. I took a wonderful walk on the beach and saw an eagle standing on the sand. I thought of Gus, and realized seeing our national bird was a great way to remember to honor the soldiers who had died for us. I got really close and took a picture. This was the first time in five months I've seen the eagle on the beach.

Then as I walked farther, I saw a hawk feather on the beach. I've been asking Gus to give me signs if he's coming back.

Jim and I learned there are new US restrictions from the Centers for Disease Control on when an overseas facility can ship pups from a litter. Apparently, in some European countries, many more lost dogs are being rescued and some are likely carrying diseases. Breeders have more control, so there is no risk associated with obtaining pups from them, but the new rules apply to everybody. The litter we are waiting for from Zsófi's Hera is supposed to be born the first or second week of June. But because of the new rules, the cutoff date to have them flown to the US would be August 1. If we don't decide to do it then, according to the rules, we'd have to wait six months more — until sometime in December. Jim and I definitely feel we should move forward, and everything will fall in place. I don't want to control it all — I want to leave it to Gus!

I'm curious whether Gus has told Sunny whether he will reincarnate soon.

I went again to the beach in the afternoon, where I saw a juvenile gator running from the marsh into the ocean. I know they dive into the surf to get the parasites off their bodies. When I turned around and walked back, the current had washed the gator all the way down to where I was. It was beached, looking a little confused, but seemed okay. I got some great pictures.

This morning, as always, I went over to watch the sunrise and talk to Gus. I told him again that I need some signs, then I spied a pair of possums running along the fence line, one behind the other. I had to laugh because it made me think of when Gus and I used to chase each other on this beach.

June 1, 2024

I woke up feeling really good. There was something special about the whole day. I fed the birds and sensed I was giving them energy, as well as connecting with nature, as is my ritual every morning and evening. Both Jim and I were talking again about whether we should get a puppy from Zsófi. There is another litter coming from the mating of Dakota and Neo, also Zsófi's dogs. To aid our decision, Jim and I drew oracle cards. Jim asked whether we should get a puppy and drew "Over the Edge." I asked whether Gus was coming back and I drew "Peace." Then I drew another card, "Soulmate." Later in the afternoon, Jim and I were still discussing it, still indecisive. We had told Zsófi we'd reply to her either yesterday or today.

We decided to draw oracle cards again. I drew "Soulmate" again. This time, Jim drew a different card, but we felt its message applied more to his business than our choice of a dog. Perhaps because I'd gotten "Soulmate" twice, we emailed Zsófi to let her know we'd love to have a male puppy from Extreme and Hera. We also told her that if Hera did not have any males, we would wait for another litter or choose a puppy from Dakota's litter, expected next week.

After we sent the email, we saw a hawk fly by with something in its talons. We felt good about our decision, and also a little nervous.

June 2, 2024

I woke up, did my ritual, and decided to wait before checking my emails to see if we heard back from Zsófi. Then Jim and I sat down together and opened her response. She'd sent pictures of her with Hera's newborn puppies. She had sent them yesterday, and we thought it was very interesting that we had made the decision before we knew the puppies had been born. We were very excited because Hera had had only four males but seven females.

I went back into the bedroom and turned on the music. The second song that came on was "Over the Rainbow." I knew this was a great confirmation from Gus because I was thinking about him moments earlier. Jim agreed that was a thumbs up from Gus. I have to admit I'm excited but a little nervous still. We will see how the rest of the day unfolds, then we wait until the new puppy comes to us at the end of July.

I went to the Greenway to walk, and right after I sent the confirming email to Zsófi, I was thinking about Gus and telling myself I needed to trust the process, *trust the process*. Then I visualized Zsófi standing in front of the four males, asking them which one wants to live with Jim and Rebecca in the US.

JUNE 3, 2024

This morning when I woke up, I thought to myself that I still have not heard from Sunny. Tomorrow will be two weeks since my last email to her. I walked into the bathroom, and as I set my phone down, Sunny's notification on WhatsApp popped up. I thought, *Wow, what synchronicity!* I listened to her voicemail. She apologized for not getting back to me. She had been very busy.

She said Gus told her I was waiting to hear from her — and she really, really wanted to start the book.

I had asked her for dates and times for meetings, but there was nothing specific in her message. I feared this might be an indication of how challenging it might be for us to work together on the book, especially because she lives in Australia and the time difference would make it complicated. She did say she would reach out when she was ready. I am more curious than ever how all of this will unfold. I resolved to let it go, for now.

I still talk to Gus, and I feel he shows me signs when numbers show up. Like today when I happened to glance at my phone, 11:11, 12:12, and 2:22 showed up. I also saw a single feather on my walk today. Such a beautiful gift, Gus! I'm so grateful — waiting for your return.

JUNE 9, 2024

Today was the wedding. It was a beautiful ceremony at Eden at Gracefield in Walterboro, South

Carolina. The oak trees there are 200-300 years old and magnificent. Before the ceremony, I felt a need to walk around and embrace myself in the energy of the trees. I held the thought that here was the land of our ancestors. I wanted them to bless the ceremony and give Alan and Lauren their blessings.

On the trip to the ceremony, I took my pucucho, which is a talisman made of baby llama's fur. It's the most powerful tool a shaman has for healing. [The Peruvians only use this fur if the animal died a natural death. They never kill it.] I have learned to use the pucucho during my healing practice as I call on Pachamama [the spirits] during ceremonies.

I walked all around the plantation grounds [where the wedding was held], feeling the energy of the land and the ancestors. Yesterday, I had affirmed in my mind that I wanted to find a feather for the ceremony, and I did find one. I also found two beautiful small white stones, which I would use as well.

I went up to the place where the ceremony would be held. Nobody was there yet. I said a blessing and a request to bring in the ancestors, the spirit guides, and everyone who wanted to be there in spirit form. I laid a stone on either side of the Christian cross where Lauren was going to stand with Alan.

As I approached the cross, a butterfly seemed to come out of nowhere, touched me on the arm, and flew away. Then a crow landed on the tree beside the cross and began to caw joyfully. I felt the presence of spirit was a confirmation that the wedding was going to be blessed.

When I did the blessing, I recorded it as a video on my phone. I plan to send it to Alan and Lauren later, after they are settled and rested.

It was a very magical day, and much of the magic for me was just from walking around. I felt at one with all the elements on this huge plantation. I was excited to find another healing stone, which will be one of the twelve stones I will need for my coursework.

That evening when we went to dinner, I realized I had left my phone at the hotel. When we returned, I saw that Sunny had texted me. She wanted to know if I had time for a quick chat. However, because I was pressed for time preparing for the wedding festivities, I was reluctant and didn't respond right away. Eventually I scheduled a time with her tomorrow.

It's been more than two weeks since she reached out about the book. She hadn't hinted about what she wanted to say, so we will see how things unfold.

One thing is for sure, I definitely felt Gus's presence when I was walking around the plantation.

June 11, 2024

Sunny and I had a call scheduled for 7:15 this evening. I waited for thirty minutes and she finally called. It felt like she was not respecting my time, and I was annoyed, but we had a good conversation. I was very open and honest with her about my feelings of uncertainty. I admitted I feel somewhat entangled with her. She has these vivid communications with Gus, and I depend on her for the transcripts of those messages. I don't understand whether Gus is literally speaking to her or she is somehow translating, putting his thoughts into her own words. It was a frank discussion, and she said she appreciated my honesty. She said, "Rebecca, if you don't trust the process or you don't trust me, that is fine. There is no judgment. I totally understand." And we ended the call.

I don't know what to make of it. I'm still confused, wondering whether I still want to be involved with her in the book project.

June 12, 2024

I woke up and did my usual ritual. I went over to the beach house, sat there, and told myself I can't do this on my own, that I need help, then a crow came flying right over my head. When I see a crow, I know it's giving me a message and helping me out. Still felt kind of funky that day but I knew I had to trust the whole process. When we were at the beach house, the crows were in the tree, cawing away. Nonstop. It made me feel like Gus was right there, saying, *I'm going to be back; I'm going to be with you.*

JUNE 13, 2024

I woke up feeling really good. I didn't have the heavy energy I'd felt yesterday. It was lighter as I sensed the spirits I'd called on were helping me out and working with me. The energy had really shifted.

I had a wonderful session with Steven. He helped me understand a lot of things about the book, about the ceremony, and the emojis that appeared on my phone when I was doing a dictation on the beach. He told me what he thought the emojis meant.

It was a good day for me. I felt the strong need to go walk on the beach. It was super windy, but the energy there was magical. The waves were rough, but talking to Gus and being with nature warmed my heart.

I saw an eagle fly out of the marsh. I knew this was a sign from Gus because I haven't seen an eagle there this trip. Also, when I was talking to Steven on the phone about Sunny and the book, crows alighted on a tree and were cawing away. Steven told me to stop and ask the crow what its message was.

The message I sensed was that Gus would be coming back. It was remarkable that the crows cawed when I was talking to Steven, then suddenly they went quiet. They were making their point!

I love how nature communicates and gives us messages. I am so grateful for it!

June 17, 2024

Today when I came back home after walking on the beach, I went into the backyard and chatted with Gus. I was alone in the house, and because it felt so empty, I was missing him even more. Thinking music might help soothe my mood, I set Pandora to "Easy Listening." The first song that came on was

"Over the Rainbow." It brought tears to my eyes. I knew Gus was with me, and the house didn't feel so empty anymore.

JUNE 27, 2024

Neither Jim nor I slept well this morning. Last night we'd been looking at videos on how to train a puppy, and we were thinking about all the responsibility. We still really wanted one, but we worried it would change our lifestyle and we might not be ready. Although we had told Zsófi our preferences, we hadn't given her the final okay. Jim and I agreed we would make the decision today or over the weekend because Zsófi needed a firm commitment before the August 1 cutoff date.

I went on my run thinking about these things. Jim and I had the idea we should mentally rehearse our daily routine as though the puppy were living with us. Then I had an idea that I would reach out to Monica, another medium I trust, to see if she could do a reading today.

I got the sense that Gus would be coming back on the first anniversary of his passing. That would be December 7, a date that would coincide with the earliest we could receive the puppy if we decided now to wait past the first of August. This made me think we should inform Zsófi that we want the puppy for sure, but I wondered if she could wait until he was six months old before sending him to us.

Then the timing of messages with Monica moved at a fast pace. She texted me, asking to see pictures of both Gus and the puppy we were considering. Her schedule would permit some time today, but to make it, there would have to be time for us to send the pictures and for her to study them. And if we couldn't manage it, her next available appointment would be after August 1 — an impossibility in this situation!

Jim and I scrambled for it. He helped me find and send the pictures.

Then when I had the session that day with Monica, she said Gus told her it was too soon, and that her sense of his returning in December was more likely. She added that he told her a sign of his return would be my finding a red feather.

Sunny had told me it was usually one to two years before animals reincarnate, so Gus's return this December would perhaps be a year early. But, again, I resolved I would let things unfold as they would.

I went down to the river this afternoon and was thinking about the red feather. I had never told Monica about my sightings of red-tailed hawks.

Tonight, Jim and I conferred as I wrote the email to Zsófi, confirming we want the puppy, but requesting that she please wait until December to send him.

JUNE 28, 2024

I woke up wondering how Zsófi would respond to our email. Then, here it came: She would hold that puppy for us and train it for six months. Wow, it's a miracle how everything is lining up!

Today when I ran on the Greenway and was thinking about Gus, I saw a small turtle, then I saw the same snake twice.

Definitely a lot of messages!

JULY 1, 2024

This morning I woke up feeling really off. I wasn't feeling balanced, but I thought I'd go ahead and do what I normally do. I fed the birds, took care of our cat Samantha, and strolled into the woods to be with the trees. I talked with the trees and walked barefoot in the grass, then came back up and sat on the patio for a bit.

I still couldn't shake the dark mood, so I decided I'd run. As I was suiting up for it, I turned on Pandora and "Over the Rainbow" came on. I knew Gus was right there with me trying to say, *It's okay, Mommy. I'm here with you.* It warmed my heart so much!

Then I went to the Greenway and ran. I found a feather on the sidewalk. It was not a red one — the predicted sign of Gus's return — but I took it as a confirmation that *Yes, Gus, it's all okay.*

To you, readers:

Later, in August, when I was walking in our garden, I found a red cardinal feather in our backyard, near the bird feeder. I knew this was it, but when I put that feather with the others I'd collected, I saw I already had a red one, also from a cardinal. I was taken aback, feeling like this was what Gus must've been talking about — a double message!

July 14, 2024

Today Donald Trump was shot but survived. Astrologically, he's a Gemini, like my father — and today is the same day my father died by suicide.

July 15, 2024

Jim and I are back at our beach house. When I was running, I saw a little flock of turkeys. I thought how sweet it would be if they would drop a feather for me. When I got close and they scurried away, I found a turkey feather. What a blessing and a gift! I was also missing Gus today.

Later, when I went to watch the sunset at the beach, I was talking to him and felt really emotional, missing him so much.

Since we're watching my daughter's dog Stella, I took her for a walk on the beach. It was the first time I had her there without Gus. I used to love to watch them run around and go in the water, so I was feeling nostalgic.

Today, we are flying back to Atlanta with Stella. As we were about to leave this house, Pandora switched on, playing "Over the Rainbow." I immediately melted and felt so grateful that Gus was listening to me. Jim and I exchanged looks of confirmation and awe. We realized Gus was saying his spirit is here with us.

July 17, 2024

We've had Stella with us since last Saturday. We brought her back to Atlanta — and boy, have we seen Gus's energy through her! Yesterday she ran for the bully stick, then she jumped in the pool to swim, like Gus used to do. It was unbelievable because I've never seen her do that. The pool was his thing. Then that afternoon, Jim did his routine with her. She chased after the stick, ran into the yard, came back with it, threw it in the pool, jumped in and fetched it, then threw it back out in the yard, also like Gus used to do. Jim and I were in awe of how she was picking up Gus's energy and it was surging through her.

Then she did the same thing today!

As Jim and I were walking through the kitchen, we noticed the tennis ball on the front edge of Gus's bed, and his favorite toy — a plush lamb — was propped on the back edge of his bed, as if staring at us. We both thought that was weird. We didn't recall seeing those toys there before. Not only had Stella recently placed that ball and the lamb there, but she'd also pushed a towel off Gus's doggie bed so she could prop up the lamb to face us. Gus was saying, *I'm here channeling through Stella.*

Later when I ran on the Greenway, I was thinking

of Gus, and there was a beautiful feather lying in the middle of the trail.

We'll see what else unfolds!

JULY 22, 2024

I woke up feeling strange with heavy energy. I wasn't sure what this strangeness was all about. I couldn't shake it. I sat outside and had the strong sense Gus said to me, *When you see another dog and they come up to you and are happy, you will know that's me. I can always soul-dog another dog to let you know I am near.*

I went to the Greenway to run. On my way, I kept asking Gus to show me what is going on and to help me relieve this heavy energy.

As I started down the Greenway, I came across an Asian couple with a black Labrador, who stopped, turned around, ran up to me, and gave me big kisses, licking my bare legs, so happy to see me. I knew immediately it was Gus's energy coming through that dog. As I started to walk away, I thanked them for letting me interact with their dog, but the dog ran after me, pulling the guy along by the leash. We all laughed. I stopped, and the dog lay down on the sidewalk to let me pet his belly. This encounter lifted my spirit so much.

That evening, Jim and I were talking about the new puppy and wondering when we would learn which one had been chosen for us. Then we received an email from Zsófi saying, "Meet your puppy!" His name is Mr. Green, and he is the one who had captured my eye months ago.

We are beyond thrilled!

July 23, 2024

I got an email from Zsófi after asking her about Mr. Green's personality. She said he is the mildest-mannered one. His pedigree name is Zöldmáli-Hunter Varazs (which means *magic*). It just so happened that Hunter was one of the names we were thinking about naming Mr. Green!

I went running down by the river and was thinking how magical and synchronized this whole process has been. A hawk showed up, and I knew it was a confirmation from Gus.

Here's puppy Hunter on Zsófi's farm before he was sent to us. They called him "Mr. Green." (Photo courtesy Zsófi Miczek)

Then I was visualizing Hunter running up to me as I was calling him, and I looked up to see a different hawk flying low above me. I knew this was another affirmation that Gus is going to soul-dog Hunter.

AUGUST 6, 2024

I emailed Sunny:

Curious how you know if an animal has reincarnated?

Sunny replied:

I have to communicate with the transitioned animal. They tell themselves if anything is changing, but the pet parents normally start having an urge to get a new pet or begin looking for one around that time. The transitioned soul makes them want to do something about that void.

I replied:

Ah, interesting. When you have time and are ready, I would greatly appreciate you communicating with Gus about this. Please let me know what he says. There is a lot I can share, but I want to hear what he knows. Thank you.

From My Journal

AUGUST 24, 2024

I wrote:

I just got through listening to Karen Anderson's recent podcast. She talks about how animals can communicate to their owners in the afterlife through digital technology, such as phones and computers, because it's all energy. I found it interesting given that Gus has sent me text messages on my phone at the most appropriate times.

15

ALL CREATURES GREAT AND SMALL

Communicating with Gus — and continuing to be mentored by him — has opened up many more paths on my spiritual journey. Perhaps that's why he was here. If that's true, my karmic debt to him goes far beyond simply helping me heal. He was — and is — helping me heal others.

As you no doubt noticed, the conversations with Gus first paralleled my own health challenges, then the evolution of my own healing practice. With the prevalence of animal extinctions and threats to the health of the planet itself, I feel as though the animals are speaking to us. Is this happening more than ever before? Or is it just that humans haven't been listening?

Perhaps animals are urging us to action. A remarkable example is the life story of my friend and colleague Georja Umano, who is an author and wildlife conservation activist.

When I told her I was writing this book, Georja told me this very intimate story about her past life:

> Years ago, I visited a hypnotherapist when I experienced a lingering pain in my back from an accident. The therapist took me back in time to the moment of the accident, and I remembered that my friend, who was with me, screamed when it happened. He coached me to tell her the fall wasn't that bad. I was okay. I was able to release the pain.
>
> So I returned to this wonderful healer when I was experiencing emotional problems. To go back to the origin of the issue, he took me back in time to my childhood and beyond. He said, "Let's delve into it. Let's see how far back the issue started in your life." So he got me very relaxed, and he said, "I'll count backward. When you get to the age when this issue happened, your little

pinky will pop up. You're not going to make it pop up. It's just going to do it by itself." He started counting down, from my age all the way back — ten, nine, eight — and when he got down to one, then he said, "Zero!" My finger popped up! I jumped out of my chair. I experienced the most vivid scene. I was in Africa. I escaped from a hunter who had killed my mother, and I was running and running through the jungle. There was a herd of elephants in the distance. They beckoned to me. They brought me into their herd. It was so vivid, it seemed like it was happening right there in the room.

This was years before I was an animal activist, and it was so real. At first, I assumed I was a little boy. But much later, when I thought about it, I realized I had to have been a baby elephant! Elephants are known for saving and fostering other animals, especially of their own family.

This experience later inspired Georja's commitment to wildlife conservation in Africa. She supports Sheldrick Wildlife Trust in Kenya, an organization that rescues baby elephants, many of them orphaned by poachers. She recently lived and worked in Kenya, where she developed a conservation education program for unwed human mothers.

Today Georja is cofounder of Elephant Matriarch Project, a conservation education center for young moms in rural areas.

Georja says:

> The elephant matriarch is the model for the program. We will ensure young mothers can continue their education and become conservation leaders in their communities — instrumental in preventing poaching and human-wildlife conflict.

Georja's story is another example of how animals are urging us to evolve, to be responsible custodians of our planet, and to expand the compassion they show us to all beings.

For a long time, even before Gus came into my life, I have set an intention to go into shamanism. I have believed that performing healings is a significant part of my soul contract. When he was with me, I'd already begun my studies, but my passion was ignited more after his death. And as you can see in Sunny's messages from him, as the emotions got deeper, he urged me on, even making it clear that if I held back and didn't pursue my practice, somehow his own soul contract would not be fulfilled.

I'm designating a space in our renovated beach house to be my "Zen room." I will not only meditate and pray there, but I also plan to perform healing sessions in that space.

Pulling together the transcripts of Sunny's conversations with Gus, along with my journal notes, I'm stunned to think of how much has happened since he passed from this life. And it's only been a year! He's not only urging me forward — he's also accelerating my spiritual development.

I was still working on this book when Jim and I traveled to Africa again. One evening when we were encamped in the Maasai Mara, a young man built a fire for us, and we huddled around it to ward off the chill after sundown. We were reminded of all those times we huddled around the firepit at home with Gus, sometimes also with Stella. Those are cherished moments.

I wanted to capture (or, recapture) that special moment, so I took a photo. I'm reproducing it here. It was only later when I studied it that I saw images in the dancing flames. And because my emotions were stirred so strongly in that moment, I wondered whether the images were a sign.

I saw faces in the flames of the African campfire.

I sent the photo to Steven Farmer. He's been encouraging me as I pursue the practice. Steven agreed there was powerful symbolism here.

Steven offered his interpretation:

> I see a tortoise who has been ignited. Tortoises are about taking your time, moving slowly; however, something has set a fire on her, yet she continues to move forward. That spark or those sparks are what will be happening to you soon — a fire of passion that won't contradict the slower pace necessarily, but will bring that "spark" more strongly into your awareness.

Again, there is the notion of being urged forward — and of not being anxious about the pace or any challenges along the way.

As Gus continues to do, Steven urged me:

> Do not fear the fires of your passion. Let go of any false pretenses that you are somehow not enough for the tasks that have been and will be put before you that are of service to the world and will inspire others — not only your writing, but your love, care, and enthu-

siastic connections and communications with your guides. You have been preparing for this for some time now, though not always consciously. Gus is a messenger for you now, and your love for this being will abide no matter what, yet the tasks before you need additional support from other guides who have assisted you.

I'm so thankful to have this encouragement and support!

It's not just the sightings of hawks and eagles - but also the uncanny timing. It was all the more meaningful for me because 2+5 = 7 and that's the day in December Gus died.

Yesterday I was on our top deck at the beach house waiting for our outdoor furniture to be delivered. One piece is a lounge. I remembered how Gus and I loved sitting on this and watching the sunset. As I was leaning against the railing and reflecting, I asked Gus, "How do you like it?" All of a sudden, a hawk flew into the tree right in front of me — no more than six feet away. I was stunned, in awe.

May you be ever surrounded by love — and may you see signs!

As Gus gazed at the sunset over the marsh, I imagined he was thinking about how much we'd achieved - and all we have left to do!

16
BOOK CLUB DISCUSSION QUESTIONS

1. Do you believe in the afterlife?
2. Have you ever received messages from your deceased beloved pet? If so, what was your experience?
3. What are your thoughts on reincarnation?
4. Do you see signs or get messages from animals around you? Do you get messages from departed ones?
5. When you receive a message from your deceased pet or a person who has transitioned, where do you feel it in your body? Does it feel like a sudden download? Like an *aha* moment?
6. Do you believe a dog can "soul-dog" another pet, but not completely take over

the body? Might it "blow out the circuits" in the dog who is alive?

7. Have you seen a living dog behave in a similar manner to a deceased one, making it seem as though a spirit might be coming through it?
8. Do you feel your thoughts or intuition can manifest your reality?
9. Do you believe a dog could come back as a human or vice versa?

17
FOR FURTHER READING

- Karen A. Anderson, *The Amazing Afterlife of Animals: Messages and Signs From Our Pets on the Other Side*
- Carl Safina, *Beyond Words: What Animals Think and Feel*
- Georja Umano, *Terriers in the Jungle: A Novel*
- Kari Weil, *Thinking Animals: Why Animal Studies Now?*

ABOUT THE AUTHOR

Author photo by Marion Yarger-Ricketts.

Rebecca Schaper is an author, filmmaker, philanthropist, and healer. *Roses to Rainbow* is her second soulful memoir. With Kyle Tekiela, she codirected and executive produced the award-winning documentary *A Sister's Call* about her mission to bring her brother Call Richmond Jr. back from the depths of homelessness and schizophrenia. She wrote about that experience in her book *The Light in His Soul: Lessons from My Brother's Schizophrenia*. About that book, Jim Hayes of the National Alliance on Mental Illness said, "This delightful story is a must-read for anyone who loves another soul living with mental health issues . . . Recovery really can happen. Read this story and leave with hope!"

Learn more at www.rebeccaschaper.com.

www.ingramcontent.com/pod-product-compliance
Lightning Source LLC
Chambersburg PA
CBHW070531090426
42735CB00013B/2940